# A Master Class with Warren Buffett and Charlie Munger

The Q&A Sessions of the Berkshire Hathaway Inc.
Shareholders' Meeting

## 2016

by

Eben Otuteye, PhD
and
Mohammad Siddiquee, PhD

**Cover Design:** Rob Williams, Graphic Designer at www.fiverr.com/cal5086

ISBN 13: 978-1544132938
ISBN 10: 154413293X

**Disclaimer:** This book is for educational purposes only. These notes are not verified or approved by Warren Buffett, Charlie Munger, nor by any director or officer of Berkshire Hathaway Inc. We relied primarily on our handwritten notes from the meeting. This publication is not meant to offer investment advice. No part of the information in this book should be considered a recommendation to purchase or sell any security.

**Authors in front of Warren Buffett's residence in Omaha**
**Photo credit: Alim Mirza**

# Table of Contents

# Preface

There is no question that Warren Buffett and Charlie Munger are investment legends of our time. Over the years they have demonstrated that they are not only great investment and business managers but that they are also sages with tremendous amount of worldly wisdom that will help people to navigate life successfully.

There are countless books written about Warren Buffett and Charlie Munger's investment style and investment success. However, there are very few sources to get their thoughts and words as directly expressed by them. Usually, you get those from interviews, newspaper or magazine articles, or more directly from the annual letter to shareholders. One rich, but generally overlooked and not well-documented source of Buffett-Munger wisdom is the question and answer sessions of the annual general meeting.

The Annual General Meeting of Berkshire Hathaway shareholders is one forum where Warren Buffett and Charlie Munger generously share their knowledge and insights on various topics. Thus, if anyone is looking for a shortcut to Buffett-Munger wisdom in investment, business, and life, the best advice is to go the Berkshire Shareholders Meeting or to get the transcript of the question and answer sessions — and is that what you get from this book.

## Motivation for Writing the Master Class Series

As professors of Finance who have taken a number of business courses and now teach a number of courses in Investments and Personal Financial Planning, we have felt and lived with a sense of dissatisfaction with the traditional academic models of investment and the methods of teaching for a long time. After we discovered the works of Ben Graham and the practice of investment by Warren Buffett, Charlie Munger and several other value investors, it became clear to us that the traditional finance curriculum in academia is shortchanging our students (the next generation) in a big way. We then took it upon ourselves to do a thorough study of the investment philosophy and practices of legendary value investors, especially Warren Buffett and Charlie Munger. In the process, we came know about this annual event called the Berkshire Hathaway shareholders meeting.

Being relatively new to Berkshire Hathaway shareholders meeting, we thought we could prepare ourselves by reading some material on it. Apart from Warren Buffett's letters to shareholders and the Berkshire annual reports, the main resource we consulted was the book *Pilgrimage to Warren Buffett's Omaha* by Jeff Mathews, which gave us quite a good orientation. In the process, we realized that there's no reliable and readily available source to access the actual Q&A sessions of past shareholders' meetings. It is our opinion that majority of those who attend the meeting are keen and teachable learners who will appreciate a reference source to review the questions and answers of the meeting. Hence, the motivation for this book. We hope both Warren Buffett and Charlie Munger will stick around for a while and maintain this format of the annual meeting in order to give us the opportunity to continue to tap into their insight and wisdom.

Another motivation for the book is that since both of us came to know about Warren Buffett and Charlie Munger rather late, we figured the way to make up for this is to introduce our students very early in their business education to the ideas of these legendary investors. Writing this series is our way of contributing to the efforts of those who are committed to spreading the word about the right way to invest, to think about money, and to manage businesses. We hope to use this *Master Class* series as the means to disseminate the ideas of Warren Buffett and Charlie Munger as directly enunciated and articulated by them. We believe it will be a great service not only to the investment community but to society in general.

Eben Otuteye
Mohammad Siddiquee
April 2017

## About the Title of the Book

On May 6, 2014, Bill Gates posted a blog[1] that began:

"In the arts, a master class is a group lesson with an acknowledged expert—a chance for students to hear from an undisputed master and to improve their work by being exposed to the best.

This last weekend, I joined almost forty thousand other 'students' to attend the master class for investors that is the Berkshire Hathaway annual meeting."

That blog resonated immediately with us and we decided to use the title of the blog as the title of this book. The Berkshire Hathaway AGM is indeed a master class with legends.

## Accuracy of Content

As those who attend the AGM are aware, part of the protocol is that no electronic recording equipment is permitted. Thus everything you read here was first handwritten. Although we tried to transcribe what was said as accurately as possible, we weren't able to make a verbatim copy. A number of expressions are paraphrases of what was actually said. However, we've made every effort to preserve the sense and meaning of what was said. We also consulted a

---

[1]    http://www.gatesnotes.com/About-Bill-Gates/Master-Class-with-Warren-Buffett-Berkshire-Hathaway-Annual-Meeting-2014

number of other attendants to cross-check our notes. While our words are not always identical to others', we are satisfied that the content is an accurate representation of what was said. Of course, the punctuation is entirely our creation.

# Berkshire Hathaway 2016 Annual Shareholders' Meeting Notes

Saturday, April 30, 2016
CenturyLink Center
455 North 10th Street, Omaha NE 68102

---

# Preliminaries

## Opening Multimedia Show

The meeting started with a video in which Warren Buffett welcomed the shareholders to the meeting. This is a multimedia extravaganza that precedes the actual meeting.

Berkshire Hathaway shareholders' meeting is popularly known as the "Woodstock of Capitalists." So, we know it is not all business. In fact, it is a weekend party of believers in the ideas, values and investment practices of Warren Buffett and Charlie Munger.

The tradition is to kick things off with some entertaining movie prior to the question and answer session.

The preliminary movie is a combination of recap of segments of the history of Berkshire, together with a series of interviews, snippets to showcase either entire Berkshire Hathaway companies (subsidiaries) or individual products, in addition to skits, parodies, cartoons, and real acting by the actual people whose stories are being told to reflect the history and values of the leadership, and in some cases poke fun at personal quirks of leaders of the company. The highlights included events specifically relevant to Berkshire Hathaway in 2016.

The preliminary show also has a serious side to it. One of the well-known values of the leadership of Berkshire is that reputation is everything (addressed several times in the questions later on). In that spirit, the preliminaries usually end with Warren Buffett's opening statement before the Subcommittee on Telecommunications and Finance of the Committee on Energy and Commerce of the U.S. House of Representatives in September 1991: "Lose money for the firm and I will be understanding; lose a shred of reputation for the firm and I will be ruthless."

## Q&A Format

The format of the Q&A session was similar to the last six annual meetings. Three business journalists—Andrew Ross Sorkin (CNBC and *New York Times*), Becky Quick (CNBC), and Carol Loomis (formerly with *Fortune Magazine*)—chose one-third of the questions. The rest came from shareholders and analysts. Shareholders had e-mailed over two thousand questions to the journalists, who then selected a set of questions most relevant to Berkshire and its operations.

The journalists, who were seated on the stage, alternated with analysts Cliff Gallant (Philadelphia Financial), Gregg Warren (Morningstar), and Jonathan Brandt (Ruane, Cunniff & Goldfarb) and with shareholders in the audience in asking the questions.

---

## Preliminary Remarks from Warren Buffett

**Warren:** Good morning. I'm Warren Buffett. This is Charlie Munger. I'm the young one. You may have noticed in the movie, incidentally, that Charlie is always the one that gets the girl. He has one explanation for that, but I think mine is more accurate. As you know, every mother in this country tells her daughter at an early age, if you're choosing between two very old and very rich guys, pick the one that's older.

We are webcasting this for the first time.[2] I'd like to welcome our visitors from all over the world. We are having this meeting simultaneously translated into Mandarin. That poses certain problems for me and Charlie because I'm not sure how sensible all our comments will come out once translated into Mandarin, but I'm not so sure how sensibly they come out initially sometimes. We are delighted to have people around the world joining us. Now the drill for the day is I'll make a couple of introductions and we will show a couple of slides and then we will go onto questions from both our two panels and from the audience; we will rotate them. We will do that until about noon. Actually, about a quarter to twelve, I will give you a rundown about a bet that was made that we report on every year. I will also, in connection with that, explain - and it ties in with it -

---

[2] For the second year, Yahoo will webcast the May 6 meeting, going live at 9 am central Time. You can watch the live stream at the following link: https://finance.yahoo.com/brklivestream

what I really think is probably the most important investment lesson in the world. We will have that about a quarter to twelve and I hope that keeps you around. Then we will break at noon for an hour for lunch. We will reconvene at one o'clock and proceed until 3:30 with questions. We will then adjourn for fifteen minutes and at 3:45 begin the formal meeting.

I'd like to make a couple of introductions. I hope Carrie Sova is here. Do we have a spotlight? Carrie puts this whole meeting together. There she is - Wonder Woman. Carrie joined us as a receptionist about six years ago and I kept throwing more and more problems at her. She put together the 50th anniversary book which we actually expanded further this year. We have a revised edition.[3] Charlie and I autographed 100 of them; we dispersed them among the group being sold. Carrie, while doing that, had a young baby girl, her second baby late in January. She has gone ahead to put on this whole annual meeting. It's a remarkable achievement I really want to thank her. It has been terrific. [applause]

We have one surprise guest. I think my youngest great-grandchild, who is about 7 months old, is also here today. If he happens to break out crying a lot, don't let it bother you. It's just his mother explaining to him my views on inherited wealth.

---

[3] You can order a copy here:
http://www.explorist.io/blog/2015/4/28/berkshire-hathaway-50th-anniversary-print-book

We also have our directors with us, they are here in the front row. If they will stand when I introduce them. Withhold your applause no matter the extreme urge is to applaud them individually. When we have finished then you can go wild.

First of all Howard Buffett [President of Buffett Farms], Steve Burke [CEO of NBCUniversal], Sue Decker [former President of Yahoo! Inc.], Bill Gates [Co-Chair of the Bill and Melinda Gates Foundation], Sandy Gottesman [Senior Managing Director of First Manhattan Company], Charlotte Guyman [former Chairman of the Board of Directors of UM Medicine], Tom Murphy [former Chairman of the Board and CEO of Capital Cities/ABC], Ron Olson [Partner of the law firm of Munger, Tolles & Olson LLP], Walter Scott [Chairman of Level 3 Communications] and Meryl Witmer [Managing member of the General Partner of Eagle Capital Partners L.P.], and that's our wonderful group. [applause].

"I did decide fairly early in my life that my favorite
employer was myself."
Warren Buffett

"When our circumstances changed, we changed our
minds."
Charlie Munger

"Looking back, I don't regret that I didn't make more
money or become better known or any of those
things. I do regret that I didn't wise up as fast as I
could have. There's a blessing in that, too. Now that
I'm 92, I still have a lot of ignorance left to work on."
Charlie Munger

# FIRST QUARTER RESULTS

I have two slides to show you now. The first one is preliminary summary figures for the 1ˢᵗ quarter.

**Berkshire Hathaway Inc.**
**Preliminary First Quarter After-Tax Earnings**
**(in millions)**

|  | 2016 | 2015 |
|---|---|---|
| Insurance – underwriting | $ 213 | $ 480 |
| Insurance – investment income | 919 | 875 |
| Total insurance | 1,132 | 1,355 |
| Railroad, utilities and energy | 1,225 | 1,466 |
| Manufacturing, service & retailing | 1,266 | 1,123 |
| Finance | 311 | 289 |
| Other | (197) | 11 |
| Operating earnings | 3,737 | 4,244 |
| Investment and derivative gains/losses | 1,852 | 920 |
| Net earnings | $5,589 | $5,164 |

You will notice that insurance underwriting - these are after-tax figures by category – are down somewhat. The basic underwriting at GEICO is actually improving. We had some important hailstorms in Texas toward the end of the quarter, and we have had some since the end of the quarter, too. There were more cat (catastrophe) losses in the first quarter than there were last year.

Railroad earnings are down significantly. Railroad car loadings throughout the industry- all of the major railroads - were down significantly in the 1ˢᵗ quarter and probably will continue to be down; almost certainly will continue to be down the balance of the year.

We have two companies, which we added to the manufacturing, service and retailing segment – Precision Castparts and Duracell. But they were added during the quarter so their full earnings aren't showing in the figures.

In the other category - and I don't like to get too technical here (you should read the 10-Q when it comes out next weekend) – but when we borrow money in other currencies, and the only currency we've done that with is the Euro; but we have a fair amount of money that we borrowed in Euros. The nature of accounting is that the foreign exchange change in value each quarter is actually shown in interest expense. If the Euro goes up, we have a lot of extra interest expense shown that way. It's not a realized factor. It moves from quarter to quarter. If the Euro goes down, it offsets interest expense. It's a technicality to some extent because we have lots of assets in Europe, and they are expressed in Euros. When they go up, it does not go through the income account. It goes directly to other comprehensive income. That figure which looks a little unusual – that's the reason for it.

We always urge you to pay no attention to the figures below operating earnings. They will bounce around from quarter to quarter. We make no attempt to manage earnings in any way – to make them smoother. We could do that very easily, but that would be ridiculous. We make investment decisions solely on the basis of what we think the best investment decision is, not on the basis of how it affects earnings in any quarter or in any year.

In the 1st quarter, we completed a transaction that was begun over a year ago whereby we exchanged our Procter & Gamble stock for cash and for Duracell. That largely accounts for the large capital gain in the quarter. Those are the figures for the 1st quarter.

To illustrate what we are all about, I put up a second slide.

### Earnings Summary
### (Outstanding Share Increase During Period – 8.2%)

| Year | After-Tax Earnings (in billions) | | Year | After-Tax Earnings (in billions) | |
|---|---|---|---|---|---|
| | Operations | Investments/ Derivatives | | Operations | Investments/ Derivatives |
| 1999 | 0.67 | 0.89 | 2008 | $9.64 | $(4.65) |
| 2000 | 0.94 | 2.39 | 2009 | 7.57 | 0.49 |
| 2001 | (0.13) | 0.92 | 2010 | 11.09 | 1.87 |
| 2002 | 3.72 | 0.57 | 2011 | 10.78 | (0.52) |
| 2003 | 5.42 | 2.73 | 2012 | 12.60 | 2.23 |
| 2004 | 5.05 | 2.26 | 2013 | 15.14 | 4.34 |
| 2005 | 5.00 | 3.53 | 2014 | 16.55 | 3.32 |
| 2006 | 9.31 | 1.71 | 2015 | 17.36 | 6.73 |
| 2007 | 9.63 | 3.58 | | | $32.39 |

I started the slide in 1999. The reason being that at the end of 1998, we effected a large merger with Gen Re. At that point, we sort of entered a different era. After the 1998 merger with Gen Re, we had a little over 1.5 million A equivalent shares out. Up to that point, we had increased the outstanding shares by more than 50% over the 30 some years preceding that point. Since that time, as I note here, we have only increased the number of shares outstanding over the next 17 years by 8.2%. So, these figures represent a fairly unchanged share account since that point whereas the share account had changed quite a bit before.

In terms of operations, I've told you, our goal at Berkshire is to increase the normalized operating earnings every year. Sometimes it will turn out to be only a little bit, and sometimes we can get some fairly decent jumps. Earnings will not increase every year because there's such a thing as a business cycle. In times of a recession, we will earn less money, obviously, than in times when things are much better overall. On top of that, we are heavily into the insurance business. Earnings there can be quite volatile because of catastrophes. This chart shows you what happened to the operating earnings since that time – again, pointing out that shares outstanding have gone up very little during that period. You will notice in 2001, when we suffered significant insurance losses through 9-11, we actually were in the red in terms of operating earnings. And you will notice that the figures are very irregular, but over time – by adding new subsidiaries, by further developing the businesses, by bolt-on acquisitions, by reinvestment of retained earnings – the earnings have moved up in a very irregular fashion quite substantially. I put in also the capital gains we've achieved through investments and derivatives, and they total some $32 billion after tax, close to 50 billion pretax. Those are not important in any given year; those numbers can go all over the place. The main advantage, from my standpoint, in that $32 billion is it gives us money to buy other businesses. What we really want to focus on, what we hope is that the bigger operations 5, 10 or 20 years from now will grow substantially, partly because we retain earnings from operations, partly because our operations improve in their own profitability, partly because they make bolt-on acquisitions, partly because we have gains from securities which enable us to buy even more businesses. We don't manage earnings, as you know, to try to get any given number from quarter to quarter. We never make a forecast on earnings. We don't give out earnings guidance. We think it's silly. We do not have budgets at the parent company level. Most of our subsidiaries have budgets but they are not required to submit them to headquarters. We just focus day after day, year after year, decade after decade on trying to add earning power – sustainable and growing earning power to Berkshire.

So that's a quick summary. Now we will move on to the questions. I ask the audience that you limit your question to one question. Multiple questions have a way of sneaking in occasionally. Let's keep them to a single question. We will start off with the journalist group on my right, and we will start off with Carol Loomis.

# Questions and Answers: Part 1

# CAPITAL INTENSIVE BUSINESSES

**Q1. Carol Loomis:** Good morning. I'll make my very short little speech about the fact that the journalists (and the analysts too) have given Charlie and Warren no hint of what they are going to ask. So, they will be learning for the first time what that's going to be also. This question comes from Eli Moises. In your 1987 letter to shareholders, you commented on the kind of companies that Berkshire Hathaway liked to buy: those that required only small amounts of capital. You said, "Because so little capital is required to run these businesses they can grow while concurrently making almost all of their earnings available for deployment in new opportunities." Today the company has changed its strategy. It now invests in companies that need tons of capital expenditures, are overregulated and earn lower returns on equity capital. Why did this happen?

**Warren:** It's one of the problems of prosperity. The ideal business is one that takes no capital, but yet grows. There are a few businesses like that. We own some. We'd love to find one that we could buy for $10, $20, or $30 billion that is not capital intensive. And we may. But it's harder, and that does hurt us in terms of compounding earnings growth. Obviously, if you have a business that grows and gives you a lot of money every year and doesn't take it - it isn't required in its growth - you get a double-barrel effect from the earnings growth that occurs internally without the use of capital. Then you get the capital that it produces to go on and buy other businesses. See's Candy was a good example of that. Back when the newspaper business was good, our *Buffalo Newspaper* was a good example of that. It was making $40 million a year at one time and had no capital requirements. We could take that whole $40 million and go buy something else with it. Increasing capital acts as an anchor on returns in many ways. One of the ways is – just because of availability - it drives us into businesses that are much more capital intensive. You just saw a slide, for example, that we have a $3.6 billion investment coming up in wind generation. We pledged, overall, to have $30 billion in renewables. Anything that Berkshire Hathaway Energy does, anything that BNSF does takes lots of money. We get decent returns on capital, but we don't get the extraordinary returns on capital that we've been able to get in some of the businesses that are not capital intensive. As I mentioned in the annual report, we have a few businesses that actually earn 100% a year on true invested capital. Clearly, that's a different sort of operation than something like Berkshire Hathaway Energy which may earn 11% or 12% on capital, and that's a very decent return, but it's a different animal than the businesses that are very low capital intensity. Charlie?

**Charlie:** When our circumstances changed, we changed our minds.

**Warren:** Slowly and reluctantly.

**Charlie:** In the early days, quite a few times we bought a business that was soon producing 100% per annum on what we paid for it and didn't require much reinvestment. If we had been able to continue doing that, we would have loved to do it. When we couldn't, we went to plan B. Plan B is working pretty well and, in many ways, I sort of prefer it. How about you, Warren?

**Warren:** That's true. When something is forced on you, you might as well prefer it. We knew that was going to happen. The question is, does it lead you from what was a sensational result to a satisfactory result? We are quite happy with the satisfactory result. The alternative would be to go back to working with very tiny sums of money. That really hasn't gotten a lot of serious discussion between Charlie and me. Now to the analysts group. Jonathan.

## PRECISION CASTPARTS ACQUISITION

**Q2. Jonathan Brandt: Hi Warren. Thanks for having me again. My first question is about Precision Castparts. Besides your confidence in its talented CEO Mark Donegan, what in particular do you like about their business that gave you the confidence to pay a historically high multiple? Are there ways Precision can be even more successful as essentially a private company? For instance, are there long term investments to support client programs or acquisitions that precision can make now that**

**they couldn't realistically have done as a publicly traded entity?**

**Warren:** We completed the acquisition of Precision Castparts at the end of January this year. We made the deal last August. You covered the most important asset in your question. Mark Donegan who runs Precision Castparts is an extraordinary manager. We've seen a lot of managers over the years. I would almost rank Mark as one of a kind. He is doing extremely important work in primarily making aircraft parts. I would say there are certainly no disadvantages to him to be working for the company, being a subsidiary of Berkshire, and not being a public company. I think he would say, and I think Charlie and I would agree with him that, over time there could be some significant advantages. For one thing, he can spend 100% of his time now on figuring out better things to do with aircraft engines. It was always his first love to be thinking about that and he did spend most of his time thinking about that, but he also had to spend some time explaining quarterly earnings to analysts and perhaps negotiating bank lines and that sort of thing. His time, like all of our managers, can be spent exactly on what makes the most sense to him. Mark doesn't have to come ever to Omaha to put on some show for me in terms of justifying a billion-dollar acquisition or plan investment. He doesn't have to waste his time on anything that isn't productive. Running a public company, you do waste your time on quite a bit of stuff that isn't productive. We've taken the main asset of Precision Castparts and made him in this case even more valuable to the company. In terms of acquisitions, Precision Castparts has always made a number of them, but being part of Berkshire, there is really no limitation on what can be done. There again, his canvas has been broadened with the acquisition by Berkshire. I see no downside whatsoever. If he needs capital, I've got an 800 number. He wasn't paying much of a dividend before, but he doesn't' have to pay any dividend now. Precision Castparts will do better under Berkshire than it would have independently although it would have done very, very well independently. Charlie?

**Charlie:** In the early days, we used to make wise-ass remarks. Warren would say we buy a business that an idiot can manage, because sooner or later an idiot will. We did buy some businesses like that in the early days. They were widely available. Of course, we'd prefer to do that, but the world has gotten harder, and we had to learn new and more powerful ways of operating. A business like Precision Castparts requires a very superior management that is going to stay superior for a long time. We gradually have done more and more of that. It's simply amazing how well it works. I think to some extent we've gotten almost as good at picking superior managers as we were in the old days of picking the no-brainer businesses.

**Warren:** We would love to be able to find, but we won't be able to find them because they are very rare birds. We would love to find another 3 or 4 of a similar type business as Precision Castparts where forever they are going to be producing something where quality is enormously important, where the customer depends very heavily on them, and where the contract extends over many years and people don't simply take the low bid in order to get the gadget of one sort or another. It's very important that you have somebody there with enormous skill running the business, and their reputation among aircraft and engine manufacturers is absolutely unparalleled.

Okay now we will go to the audience and we will go up to Station 1 and if you will give your name and where you are from I'd appreciate it.

## HAPPINESS

**Q3. Shareholder, Station 1: Good morning, my name is Gaspar. I am Spanish and I come from London, I admire you both in many ways. I would like to know, looking backwards, what would you have done differently in life in your search for happiness?**

**Warren:** Well, I'm 85, and I can't imagine anybody any happier than I am. By accident or whatever, I'm sitting here eating exactly what I like to eat, doing in life exactly what I love to do with people I love. It really doesn't get any better than that. I did decide fairly early in my life that my favorite employer was myself. I think that worked out well – I managed to avoid aggravation of almost any sort. If you or those around you that you love have health problems, then that is a real tragedy. There's not much you can do about it but accept it. Charlie and I have really been blessed. Charlie is 92; he's doing every day something that he finds fascinating. He probably finds what he is doing at 92 as interesting, as fascinating, as rewarding, and socially productive, as any period you can pick in his life. We've been extraordinarily lucky. We are lucky as a partnership; it's more fun doing things as a partnership. I don't have any complaints. If you're talking about business life, I don't think I would have started with a textile company. Charlie?

**Charlie:** Looking back, I don't regret that I didn't make more money or become better known or any of those things. I do regret that I didn't wise up as fast as I could have. There's a blessing in that, too. Now that I'm 92, I still have a lot of ignorance left to work on. [applause].

**Warren:** Okay, Becky Quick.

## REINSURANCE

**Q4. Becky Quick: This question comes from Solomon Ackerman who is in Frankfurt, Germany. He wants to know why has Berkshire significantly sold down their holdings in Munich Re, which is the world's biggest reinsurance company based in Germany, while sticking with the reinsurance operations within Berkshire, like Berkshire Hathaway Reinsurance and General Re. Would you reduce exposure to Berkshire Hathaway Reinsurance or General Re if they were listed companies? And he is hoping that**

this will bring out some of your insights as to what's happening in the reinsurance business right now.

**Warren:** I said in the annual report that I thought it was very likely that the reinsurance business would not be as good in the next 10 years as it has been in the last 10 years. I may be wrong on that but that's a judgment based on seeing the competitive dynamics of the reinsurance business now versus ten or twenty years ago. We sold our entire holdings, which were substantial, of Munich Re and Swiss Re - we owned about 3% of Swiss Re and we owned more than 10% of Munich Re. Last year we sold those two holdings. They are fine companies, well-managed companies. We like the people that run them. I think the business of the reinsurance companies generally is less attractive for the next 10 years than it has been for the last 10 years in part because of what's happened to interest rates. A significant portion of what you earn in insurance comes from investment of the float. And the business of both of those companies and, for that matter almost all of the reinsurance industry, is somewhat more restricted in what they can do with their float because they don't have the huge capital cushion that Berkshire has. They also don't have the great amount of unrelated earning power that Berkshire has. Berkshire has more leeway in what it can do simply because it does have capital that's many times what its competitors have. It also has earning power coming from a whole variety of unrelated areas, unrelated to insurance. So, it was not a negative judgment in any way on those two companies or their management, but it was at least a mildly negative judgment on the reinsurance business. We have the ability at Berkshire to actually rearrange to a degree - we are certainly affected by industry factors but we have more flexibility in modifying business models and we have operated that way over the years in insurance generally and particularly in reinsurance. Munich Re, Swiss Re, and all the major reinsurance companies, except for us, are pretty well tied to a given type of business model. They don't really have as many options in terms of where capital gets deployed. They have to continue down the present path. I think they will do fine but not as fine in the next ten years as they have in the last ten years. I don't think if we played the same game as we were playing the last ten [year], we would do as well. But we do have considerably more flexibility in terms of how we conduct all of our insurance operations but particularly in reinsurance. We have an extra string to our bow that the rest of the industry doesn't have. The amount of capital that has come into the reinsurance business, it's no fun running a traditional reinsurance company and have money coming in, particularly in Europe, and look around you for investment choices and find out that many of the things you were investing in years ago now have negative yields. The whole idea of float is that it's supposed to be invested at a fairly substantial positive rate and that game has been over for a while and it looks like it will be at least unattractive, if not terrible, for a considerable period in the future. Charlie?

**Charlie:** There's a lot of new capacity in reinsurance and a lot of very heavy competition. A lot of people from finance have come over into reinsurance and all the old competitors remain, too. That's different from Precision Castparts where most of the customers would be totally crazy to hire some other supplier because Precision Castparts is so much more reliable and so much better. Of course, we like the place with more competitive advantage. We are learning.

**Warren:** To put it terms of Economics 101, basically in reinsurance, supply has gone up but demand has not gone up. Some of the supply is driven by investment managers who would like to establish something offshore where they don't have to pay taxes. Reinsurance is the easiest - sort of what you might call the beard behind which to actually engage in money management in a friendly tax jurisdiction, and you can set up a reinsurance operation with very few people by taking large chunks of what brokers may offer. It's not the greatest reinsurance in the world and a couple of the operations that have proven that statement to be right. It's a very easy way to have a disguised investment operation in a friendly tax jurisdiction, but that becomes supply in the reinsurance field and supply has gone up relative to demand and it looks to me like that will continue to be the case and couple that with poor returns on float and it's not as great a business as it used to be. Now we will talk to an insurance man about it, Cliff Gallant.

## PROGRESSIVE VS. GEICO

**Q5. Cliff Gallant:** In terms of growth and profitability, **GEICO** really got whooped by **Progressive Direct** over the last year. In 2015, **Progressive Direct** auto business group policy count up by **9.1%**, **GEICO** only **5.4%** and in terms of profitability the combined ratio at **Progressive** was a **95 to 1** and **GEICO** was a **98.0**. Is this evidence that **Progressive's** investment in technology like **Snapshot**, (investments that **GEICO** has spurned), is making a difference in a time of difficult loss trends? Why is **GEICO** suddenly losing to **Progressive Direct**?

**Warren:** I forget what year it was we passed Progressive and what year it was we passed Allstate but GEICO's growth rate in the 1st quarter was not as high as it was in the past couple of first quarters, but it was quite satisfactory. The first quarter is by far the best quarter for growth. Last year, both frequency (how often people had accidents) and severity (which is the cost per accident) went up quite suddenly and substantially. Progressive's figures show they were hit by that less than Allstate and GEICO and some others. But I don't think you necessarily will see the same trends this year. Last year, for the first time in I don't know how many years, the number of deaths and auto accidents per hundred million miles went up. If you go back to the mid-1930s, there were almost 15 people killed per hundred million miles driven. It got down to just slightly over 1 – from 15 to 1. You had roughly as many people killed in auto accidents in the mid-1930s, about 30 – 32 thousand a year as we had last year or the year before when people drove almost 15 times as many miles. Cars have gotten far, far, far safer. It's a good thing. If we had the same rate of deaths from auto accidents as we had in the 1930s relative to miles driven, we would have had a half million people die last year from auto accidents instead of a figure closer to 40,000. Last year for the first time there was more… I think there was more distracted driving so you really had this uptick in frequency, and more important, in severity. GEICO has adjusted its rates. My own prediction would be that the underwriting margins at GEICO will be better this year than last year, although you never know when catastrophes are coming along. March and April had a lot of activity. I made a bet a long time ago, a mental one, on the GEICO model versus the Progressive model. They were significantly ahead of us in volume a few years back. We passed them and Allstate. I hope on my 100th birthday that the GEICO people announce to me that they passed State Farm. I have to do my share on that by getting to 100, so we will see what happens on that particular one. Charlie?

**Charlie:** I don't think that it's a tragedy that some competitor got a little better ratio for one period. GEICO quadrupled its market share since we bought all of it.

**Warren:** Quintupled.

**Charlie:** Quintupled, alright. I don't think we should worry about the fact that someone else had a good quarter. [applause]

**Warren:** I think it's far more sure that GEICO will pass State Farm someday than I will make it to 100. I'll put it that way. Okay, we will go to the shareholders in Station 2.

## AMAZON'S COMPETITIVE THREAT

**Q6. Shareholder, Station 2: Greetings to all of you from the Midwest of Europe. I'm Norman Nimtropf from Bonn, Germany, a shareholder since 1992. My question is about the future of salesmanship in our companies. Warren, you have always demonstrated a heart for direct selling. When we met you in the midst of a tornado warning in a barbershop, you immediately offered to write insurance for us.**

**Warren:** That's true; they were all huddled down there in the barbershop. There wasn't going to be any tornado so I told them if they gave me a dollar, they could go upstairs, and if anything happened to them I'd pay them a million dollars or something like that.

**Questioner: With the rise of Amazon.com and others, we see a shift from push marketing to pull marketing. From millions of catalogs having been sent out in the past to now consumers searching on what they are looking for. What is**

**your take on how this shift from push to pull marketing will affect our companies?**

**Warren:** The development you refer to is huge, I mean really huge. It's not just Amazon but Amazon is a huge part of it. And what they have accomplished in a fairly short period of time and continue to accomplish is remarkable. The number of satisfied customers they have developed... we don't make any decision, involving even the manufacturing of goods or retailing, before thinking long and hard about what the world will look like in 5, 10, 20 years – looking at the powerful trend, hugely powerful trend you just described. We don't look at that as something we'll try to beat them at their own game. They are better than we are at that so Charlie and I are not going to outbezos Bezos by a long shot. We aren't going to think about that. It does not worry us obviously with Precision Castparts. It does not worry us in terms of the overwhelming majority of our businesses, but it is a huge economic trend that 20 years ago was not on anybody's radar screen and lately has been on everybody's radar screen. Many of them, and including us in a few areas, have not figured the way to either participate in it or counter it. GEICO is a good example of a company in an industry that had to adjust to change and some people made the change better than others. We were slow on the Internet. The phone had worked so well for us in traditional advertising that there's always a resistance to think about new possibilities. When we saw what was happening on the Internet, we jumped in with both feet. The nature of capitalism is if you've got a good business, somebody is always trying to figure out a way to take it away from you and improve on it. The full effect on the industry is far from having been seen. It is a big, big force, and it already has disrupted plenty of people and it will disrupt more. I think Berkshire is quite well situated. One big advantage we have is we didn't see ourselves starting as one industry. We didn't think of ourselves as department store guys or tire guys or steel guys. We thought of ourselves as having capital to allocate. If you start with a given industry focus and spend your whole time working on how to make a better tire, whatever it may be, I think it's hard to have the flexibility of mind that you have if you just think you have, hopefully, a large and growing pile of capital and try to figure out what is the next best move you can make with that capital and I think we do have a real advantage that way. I think Amazon has a real advantage too in this intense focus on having hundreds of millions of generally very happy customers getting very quick delivery on something they want to get promptly and they want to shop the way they want to shop. If I owned a bunch of shopping malls, I'd be thinking plenty hard about what they might look like 10 or 20 years from now. Charlie?

**Charlie:** We failed so thoroughly in retailing when we were young that we pretty well avoided the worst troubles when we were old. I think that Berkshire has been helped by the Internet. The help at GEICO has been enormous and it contributed greatly to the huge increase in market share. Our biggest retailers are so strong that they will be among the last people that have troubles from Amazon.

**Warren:** I didn't get that dollar from you Norman, after I gave you that wonderful advice. Andrew.

## COKE AND HEALTH

**Q7. Andrew Ross Sorkin:** Thank you, Warren. Great to see you today. Got a lot of questions on this particular topic and this question is a particularly pointed one. Warren, for the last several years in this meeting, you've been asked about the negative effects of Coca-Cola products and you've done a masterful job at dodging the question by telling us how much Coke you drink personally. Statistically, you may be the exception. According to a peer review study by Tufts University, soda and sugary drinks may lead to 184,000 deaths among adults every year. The study found that sugar sweetened beverages contributed to 133,000 deaths from diabetes, 45,000 deaths from cardiovascular disease, and 6,450 deaths from cancer. Another shareholder wrote in about Coke and noted that you declined to invest in the cigarette business on ethical grounds despite once saying, "It was a perfect business because it costs a penny to make, sell it for a dollar, it's addictive, and there is fantastic brand loyalty." Again, removing your own beverage consumption from the equation, please explain directly why we Berkshire Hathaway shareholders should be proud to own Coke?

**Warren:** I think people confuse the amount of calories consumed. I happen to like to consume about 700 calories a day from Coca Cola so I'm about one-quarter Coca Cola. But I think if you decide that sugar generally is something that the human race should not have… I elect to get my 26 or 27 hundred calories a day from things that make me feel good when I eat them. That is my sole test. It wasn't a test that my mother necessarily thought was great or my grandfather, but there are over 1.9 billion 8-ounce servings of some Coca Cola drinks consumed daily – they have an enormous range of products. 1.9 billion daily servings – that's 693,500,000 (693.5 billion) of 8 ounce servings a year, except it's a leap year – that's almost one hundred 8 ounce servings per capita for 7 billion people in the world every year, and that's been going on since 1886. I would find it quite spurious the fact that somebody says if you're eating 3,500 or so calories a day or you're consuming 2,700 or 2,800 and some of the 3,500 is Coca Cola then any obesity-related illness is from the Coke you drink. You have the choice of consuming more than you use, and I make a choice to get 700 calories from this. I like fudge a lot, peanut brittle. I am a very, very happy guy. I think - and I'm serious about this: but I think if you are happy every day (it may be hard to measure), you're going to live longer as well. So, there may be a compensating factor. I really wish I had a twin, and the twin had eaten broccoli his entire life, and we both consumed the same number of calories. I know I would have been happier and probably would have lived longer. I think Coke is a marvelous product. If you consume

35 hundred or 4 thousand calories a day and live a normal life in terms of your metabolism something is going to go wrong with your body at some point. I think if you balance out the calories so that you don't become obese...

I have not seen any evidence that convinces me that I'd reach 100 if I suddenly switched to broccoli and water. A friend of mine, RJ Miller, a remarkable man (became the president of Ford Motor Company), had his 100th birthday on March 4 of this year. I saw him for his birthday, and RJ told me that there were 10,000 men in the U.S. that live to be 100 or better and 45,000 women. I checked the Internet, the census figures, and sure enough, that is the ratio. If you really want to improve your longevity prospects, have a sex change. You are four and a half times more likely to get to be 100. It's just a matter of fact, folks. I think I'll have Charlie go first on that one.

**Charlie:** I like the peanut brittle better than the Coke. I drink a lot of Diet Coke. I think people that ask questions like that one always make one ghastly error that's inexcusable. They measure the detriment without considering the advantage. That's really stupid. That's like saying we should give up air travel because 100 people die a year in air crashes; that would be crazy. The benefit is worth the risk. If every person has to have 8 or 10 glasses a day of water to stay alive and it's pretty cheap and sensible and adds to life to add a little extra sugar, add a little stimulation and calories, there are huge benefits to humanity in that and it's worth having some disadvantage. We ought to have almost a law, now I'm sounding like Donald Trump, where these people shouldn't be allowed to cite the defects without citing the offsetting advantages. It's immature and stupid.

**Warren:** Okay, Gregg Warren.

## BERKSHIRE HATHAWAY ENERGY

**Q8. Gregg Warren: Warren, with both coal-fired and natural gas plants continuing to generate around two thirds of the nation's electricity and renewables accounting for less than 10%, there remains plenty of room for growth. At this point, Berkshire Hathaway Energy which has invested heavily in this segment is one of the nation's largest producers of both wind and solar power and yet still only generates around one third of its overall capacity from renewables. As you noted earlier, MidAmerican recently committed another 3.6 billion dollars to wind production, which should lift the amount of electricity it generates from wind to 85% by 2020. The company overall is pledging to have around $30 billion in renewables longer term. The recent push in renewables with both the wind and solar energy tax credits has made this kind of investments more economically viable and should clear the path for future investments. Eliminating coal fired plants looks to be the main priority but natural gas plants are also fossil fuel driven and are exposed to the vagaries of energy prices. Is the end game here for Berkshire**

Energy to get 100% of its generation capacity converted over to renewables and what are the risks and rewards associated with that effort? After all, the company operates in a highly regulated industry where rates are driven by an effort to keep customer costs low while still providing adequate returns for the utilities.

**Warren:** Any decision we make, including the one we just showed during the movie, any decision about new generation, changes in generation has to go through what is usually called the Public Utility Commission [PUC]. The utility industry is overwhelmingly regulated at the state level and we cannot make changes that are not approved by the PUC. We've had more problems, for example, in bringing in renewables in our western utility PacifiCorp because it's in effect regulated by six states. They don't necessarily agree on how the costs and benefits should be divided. If we put in a bunch of renewables then we have to follow their instructions. Iowa has been marvelous about encouraging it at every level. Consumer groups and the governor have seen the benefits. We have one major competitor called Aliant. They have not, either been able to, or - I don't know the reasons - but they have not pursued renewables the way we have. So our rates are considerably lower than theirs. If you look at their budget projections, although they have substantially higher rates than we have now they may well need a rate increase within a year or so. With our latest expansion we have said that we will not need a rate increase until 2029 at the earliest, that's 13 years.

There have been great benefits if you have a regulation that works with you on that. It is a determination that is made at the state level. The federal government has encouraged in a major way the development of renewables by this production tax credit, which currently amounts to about 2.3 cents per kilowatt-hour. We would not have the renewable generation that we have if it hadn't been for the fact that the building of those projects is subsidized by the federal government, because the benefits with reducing solar emissions or carbon emissions are worldwide and therefore, it's deemed proper that the citizenry as whole should participate in subsidizing the cost of reducing those emissions. That has encouraged, in fact, has allowed such things as happened in Iowa. But the degree to which the renewables replace primarily coal, (but there are plenty of emissions connected with natural gas if you trace it all the way through), will depend on governmental policy and, so far, I think it's been quite sensible in encouraging having the cost borne by society as a whole in terms of reduced tax revenues and seeing the benefit, which is less emissions into the atmosphere, as not limited to the people of Iowa when we build wind generation. You see, the benefit accrues to the whole world. You will see continued change. It will vary by jurisdiction. We've got the capital. We've got lots of taxes, federal taxes, paid in our consolidated return so we are in a particularly advantageous position to take advantage of massive investments that companies with limited tax appetites couldn't handle. We are in a position to be a very big player but governmental policies will be the major driver. Charlie?

**Charlie:** I think we are doing way more than our share of shifting to renewable energy. We are charging way lower prices to our utility customers and other people. If the rest of the world is behaving as we are, it will be a much better world. I will say this: I think the people who worry about climate change, the major trouble of earth, don't have my view. I like all of the shifting to renewables, but I have a different reason – I want to conserve the hydrocarbons because eventually I think we are going to use every drop for chemical feedstocks. I'm in their camp, but I have a different reason.

**Warren:** One thing you might find interesting, Nebraska has not done much with wind power. Maybe two miles from where we are sitting right across the river, people are buying their electricity cheaper in Council Bluffs, Iowa than they are in Omaha. Nebraska is entirely a public power state. The bonds are issued on a tax-exempt basis yet electricity is considerably cheaper across the river. The wind blowing does not just start at the Missouri River. It comes across Nebraska and that wind could be captured but so far it hasn't been. The real irony is because our electricity is so much cheaper in Iowa, you have these massive server firms. It's become a tech haven for these operations that gobble up electricity. Iowa has gotten plant after plant, job after job, and gotten more property tax revenues. The massive Google server firm about 8 miles from here is located in Iowa because we have cheap wind-generated electricity, and it's creating jobs. It's fascinating but Nebraska has prided itself on public power, originated back in the '30s. It has been a source of pride, but lately it has been a source of cost, too. Okay shareholder Station 3.

## DERIVATIVES

**Q9. Shareholder, Station 3: Good morning Mr. Buffett and Mr. Munger. My name is Adam Burgman. I'm with Sterling Capital in Virginia Beach. In your 2008 shareholder letter you said "Derivatives are dangerous. They have dramatically increased the leverage and risks in our financial system. They have made it almost impossible for investors to understand and analyze our largest commercial banks and investment banks." So, my question for you is how do you analyze and value companies like Bank of America and Merrill Lynch and other commercial banks that Berkshire has investments in relative to their significant derivative exposures?**

**Warren:** Derivatives do complicate the problem very dramatically. They are moving away to being collateralized which helps. But there is no question that if you asked me to describe the derivative position of the B of A, for example, I would know that they have done a conscientious job and worked hard at properly evaluating but the great danger in derivatives is if there is discontinuity. If there is no discontinuity then you probably don't have much of a problem. If the system stops for a while: it stopped after 9-11 for three or four days; it stopped during World War I; they closed the New York Stock Exchange for many months; and they debated closing the stock exchange very seriously the day after October 19, 1987. There were a lot of people that wanted to close it on that Tuesday morning but it continued. If you have a major cyber, nuclear, chemical or biological attack on the country, which will certainly happen at some point, if you have a major discontinuity then you will have a lot of problems. When things reopen, you will find there can be enormous gaps in things you thought were fully protected by collateral or netting arrangements and that type of thing. I regard very large derivative positions as dangerous. We inherited a modest size position at Gen Re in a benign market. We lost about $400 million just in trying to unwind it with no pressure on us whatsoever. So, I do think it continues to be a danger to the system.

**Charlie:** By the way the accountants blessed that big derivatives as being worth a lot of money. They were only off by what, many hundreds of millions?

**Warren:** Charlie found one position when he was on the audit committee at Salomon. I think it was mismarked by $20 million. By happenstance, I do know of one incredibly mismarked position - it does not affect any of our operations - but it almost staggers the mind to know the way that position is marked and you can only come to the conclusion that some trader got influenced, did it himself or didn't know enough. Some of these things get so complicated they are very hard to evaluate. That's the kind that have the most profit in them usually, so they were quite enthusiastic about those when we were at Salomon. They can be extraordinarily hard to mark and, like I said, I know one that was so much marked that it would blow your mind. The auditors, I don't think, are necessarily capable of holding that behavior in check. It's very interesting, because now there are four really big auditing firms. And obviously they are auditing companies where there is a derivative position and they are auditing Company A that's on one side of the transaction and auditing Company B that's on the other side, and in some cases it's the same auditor. I will guarantee you that there are plenty of times that the marks that they are attesting to are significantly different which would be an interesting exercise to pursue in terms of checking those numbers out. Derivatives are still dangerous in large quantities. We would not do them on a collateralized basis because if there was discontinuity, I don't know where we would end up. I would never get us in a position where we would have money demanded of us and not be able to fulfill it with ease and me sleeping well so we won't engage in it. We have some derivatives in runoff and, so far, we've made money and have the use of money for a decade or more. It's been very attractive for us but that does not entice me at all into doing any derivatives transactions that would involve collateral when collateral was not required. It's still a potential time bomb in the system. Anything were discontinuities -

and basically that means closing up, stopping, trading markets from functioning; anything where discontinuities can exist can be real poisonous in markets. Kuwait went into a very delayed system on settlement of stock purchases.[4] So, they didn't have to settle up for 6 months or thereabouts. It caused all kinds of problems. You have an IOU from someone for six months. If you have a zillion of those, a lot of trouble can ensue. So, I agree with your general caution. I'm not in the least troubled by our Bank of America investment nor Wells Fargo. Our Bank of America position right now is a preferred stock but we are very likely to exercise the warrants on that.[5] On the other hand, there are a great number of banks in the world. If you take the 50 largest banks in the world, we wouldn't even think about 45 of them, wouldn't you say, Charlie?

**Charlie:** We are in the awkward position where I think we will make about $20 billion out of derivatives in just those few contracts that we did years ago. We are different from the banks. We would prefer if those derivatives had been illegal for us to buy. It would have been better for our country.

---

[4] Kuwait Stock Exchange was halted on November 13, 2008 by a Kuwaiti court ruling in an effort to stop the bleeding of the 40-months low market.

[5] On August 25, 2011, Berkshire Hathaway invested $5 billion in the preferred stock of Bank of America (NYSE: BAC) yielding 6% a year plus warrants to purchase 700 million shares of Bank of America common stock at an exercise price of $7.14 per share.

**Warren:** Carol.

## FLOAT AND NEGATIVE INTEREST RATES

**Q10. Carol Loomis: This question relates to something that Warren briefly said earlier today. The question comes from Lynn Palmer who is just finishing her freshman year in a Huston Texas High School. My question, she says, concerns the float generated by Berkshire's insurance companies. In Mr. Buffett's 2015 annual letter he said that the large amount of float that Berkshire possesses allows the company to significantly increase its investment income. But what happens when interest rates decline. If the U.S. were to implement negative interest rates in the same way that the Eurozone and Japan have done, how would Berkshire be affected?**

**Warren:** Some of our float actually exists in Europe where we have the problem of negative interest rates on very high grade short-term and even medium term bonds. Obviously, anything that reduces that value of money will affect Berkshire because we will always have a lot of money. Because we have so much capital and so many sources of earning power. We have the ability, quite properly, to use our float to a certain degree in ways that most insurance companies can't think about. We can find things to do. We've got $50 odd billion of short-term government securities now and another $8.3 billion in all likelihood coming in June from Kraft Heinz preferred stock. We will be back to over $60 billion again very soon. So, we have 60 billion out that's out at ¼ of 1 percent. Well, the difference between a ¼ percent and minus ¼ of one percent is not that great. It's almost as painful to have 60 billion out at a ¼ of a percent as to have it out at a negative rate. Float is not worth as much to insurance companies now, with lower interest rates, as it was 10 or 15 years ago. That's true at Berkshire. It's worth considerably more to us than it is to typical insurance companies because we have a broader range of options as to what to do with it. There's no question about that. Having lots of money around now is not just a problem for insurance companies; it's a problem for retirees. It's a problem for anyone stuck with fixed-dollar investments and finds their income now is a pittance or in Europe perhaps a negative rate and that was not something that was in their calculations at all 15 years ago. We love the idea, however, of increasing our float. That money has been very useful to us over time. It's useful to us today even under present conditions. It's likely to be very useful to us in the future. It's shown as a liability, but it's actually a huge asset. Charlie?

**Charlie:** I've got nothing to add.

**Warren:** He's now in full swing. Jonathan.

"When you buy a stock, get yourself in a mental frame of mind that you're buying a business. And if you don't get a quote on it for five years that's fine. You don't get a quote every day on your farm or apartment house or McDonald's franchise."
Warren Buffett

"I think if you expect a lot of financial efficiency in American higher education, you are howling at the wind."
Charlie Munger

"I think if you expect a lot of financial efficiency in American higher education, you are howling at the wind."
Charlie Munger

# RAILROAD INDUSTRY AND BNSF

**Q11. Jonathan Brandt:** The railroad industry seems right now to be suffering from exposure to some of the weakest parts of the economy with volume declines of varying magnitudes in coal, oil, sand and metals. Even intermodal, usually a steady source of growth has been relatively weak as of late. How much of the weakness is cyclical, how much is secular? In the last 15 months the other western railroads market capitalization is down by 35% as projections of future growth have come down. Is your estimate of BNSF's intrinsic value down by a material amount during the same period or is your view of the value of BNSF's irreplaceable network unaffected by these short-term wiggles?

**Warren:** Certainly the decline in coal, which is about 20% of revenue, is secular. There are other factors that may cause the line of decline to jiggle around. We had a very mild winter and we went into the winter with utilities carrying unusual amounts of coal. Ironically, part of the reason for that was that our service the year before had been bad, and we got low on coal. So, they [the utilities] compensated by bringing in more than they needed just to catch up. Because the weather was mild the electricity use was poor in the wintertime. They continue at this point to have more coal on hand than they would like. They are trying to under order what they will be using and that has a little effect. The decline in coal is secular and at 20% of revenue that's a significant factor.

It's true that the market generally got very enthused about railroad stocks a year or two ago. They sold up a lot and now that people have seen that car loadings are down, and earnings are down, that things are down in some places. Equity valuations have come down in some places. We love the fact that we own BNSF. We think we bought it at an attractive price. We would love to be able to buy a second thing exactly like it at that price, we would do it in a second and pay a little bit more probably. We don't mark up and down our wholly-owned businesses based on stock market valuations. Obviously, stock market valuations are some factor in our thinking. We are not marking our wholly-owned businesses to market because we are going to hold them forever. We regard BNSF as a very good business to hold forever. But it will lose coal volume, and they will lose in some other areas and gain in other areas. It's a terrific invaluable asset that will earn a lot of money this year but not as much as last year. Charlie?

**Charlie:** I've got nothing to add.

**Warren:** Okay, Station 4.

## HOGWARTS AND VALUE INVESTING

**Q12. Shareholder, Station 4:** Hi Warren and Charlie, great to see you. This is Cora and Dan Chen from Talguard Investments of Los Angeles. This annual meeting reminds me of the magical world of Hogwarts, of Harry Potter.

This arena is our Hogwarts. Warren, you are our Headmaster and Professor Dumbledore.

**Warren:** I haven't read Harry Potter but I'll take it as a compliment.

Questioner: Charlie is our Headmaster Snape, direct and full of integrity. The magic of long term concentrated value investing is real, yet, similar to Harry Potter, the rest of the world doesn't believe we exist. Your letter to me has changed my life. Your Secret Millionaires Club[6] has changed my children's life. They go to class chatting about investing. My question is for my children watching at home today and the children in the audience. How should they look at stocks when every day in the media, they see companies that have never made a dime in their life go IPO, they are dilutive and they see a lot of short time span, the cycles getting shorter and shorter? How should they view stocks and what's your message for them? Finally, Cora and I would like to thank you in person and shake your hand personally today. I will repeat what I said last year. "Thank you for setting the seeds for my generation to sit in the shade and for my children's generation to sit in the shade with the

---

[6] Secret Millionaires Club with Warren Buffett, an animated series that features Warren Buffett as a mentor to a group of entrepreneurial kids whose adventures lead them to encounter financial and business problems to solve, http://www.smckids.com

**Secret Millionaires Club. I truly walk amongst giants. Thank you.**

**Warren:** Would you mind repeating the whole thing? We want to give great credit to Andy Heyward[7], who worked hard on "The Secret Millionaires Club." I know it has helped thousands and thousands of children and it was Andy's idea. It grows in strength and having young children learn good lessons in terms of handling money and making friendships and just generally behaving as better citizens is a great objective and Andy makes it easy for them to do. So, on his behalf, I accept your comments. You don't have to really worry about what's going on in IPOs or people making money. People win lotteries every day. You don't have to be jealous. If they want to do mathematically unsound things, and one of them occasionally gets lucky, that's nothing to worry about. They put the one winner on television, and the other million that contributed to it – with the big slice taken out for the state – don't get on; it's nothing to worry about. All you have to do is figure out what makes sense. When you buy a stock, get yourself in a mental frame of mind that you're buying a business. And if you don't get a quote on it for five years that's fine. You don't get a quote every day on your farm or apartment house or McDonald's franchise. You want to look at stocks as businesses and think about their performance as businesses. Think about what you

---

[7] Andrew A. "Andy" Heyward is the former Chairman and CEO of DIC Entertainment, an animation production company. He is currently CEO of Genius Brands International.

pay for them as you would think about buying a business. Let the rest of the world go its own way. You don't want to get into a stupid game just because it's available. I'm going to say a little more about that close to the break but with that I'll turn it over to Charlie.

**Charlie:** I think that your children are right to look for people who they can trust in dealing with stocks and bonds. Unfortunately, more than half the time they will fail, in a conventional answer. They have a really hard problem. If you just listen to your elders they will lie to you and spread a lot of folly.

**Warren:** They really have an easy problem, in the sense that American businesses as a whole will do fine over time.

**Charlie:** But not the average fund or stockbroker.

**Warren:** We will talk about that later. The stockbroker will do fine. I'll address that just a little later. A lot of problems, as Charlie would say, are caused by envy. You don't want to get envious of someone who's won the lottery or the IPO that went up. You have to figure out what makes sense and follow your own course. Becky?

## SOLAR ENERGY

**Q13. Becky Quick: This question comes from a shareholder named Elisa Kang Lee in Singapore. And it has to do with NV Energy issue with solar**

energy in Nevada. Can the Chairman help its environmentally conscious shareholders understand why NV Energy has lobbied for new rules in Nevada that make it prohibitive for households to use solar energy? Is there a good reason that we haven't yet heard about? And can the Chairman or Vice-Chairman share their views on whether there is a need to implement an environmental social and governance policy on Berkshire investments going forward? I understand that Berkshire Hathaway typically lets the underlying operating companies and CEOs manage their own policies autonomously. Should Berkshire's board influence better environmental protection policies going forward?

**Warren:** The public utility and the pricing policies in Nevada as well as other places are determined by a Public Utility Commission [PUC]. There are three commissioners that decide what's proper. The situation in Nevada is that, in terms of rooftop power, for the last few years, if you had a solar project on your roof, you could sell back the excess power you generated to the grid at a price that was far, far above what we, as a utility, could buy it for elsewhere. You could sell it back for I'll say roughly 10 cents a kilowatt-hour and about 17,000 people (maybe a few more now) had rooftop installations. Now there were federal credits involved but they got sold to other people, in terms of tax credits. They were being subsidized by the federal government and that encouraged solar generation as it has encouraged us to do solar generation and wind generation as well.

The people who had the 17,000 rooftop installations were selling back to the grid at roughly 10 cents a kilowatt hour energy that we could purchase elsewhere or produce for 3.5 cents or thereabouts. Ninety-nine percent of our consumers were being asked to subsidize the 1% that had solar units by paying triple the market price at what we could otherwise buy electricity and sell it to the other 99%. It's a question if you wish to have the 99% subsidize the 1%. The PUC in Nevada originally let this small group experiment by giving them this 10 cents rebate. They then decided the 99% should not be subsidizing the 1%. There's no question that for solar to be competitive, just like wind, it needs subsidization. The cost is not yet at a level where it becomes competitive with natural gas for example.

Who pays for the subsidy gets to be a real question, if you want to encourage people to use renewables. In general, the federal government has done it through tax subsidies which means that tax payers generally throughout the country subsidize it. The PUC in Nevada decided that after seeing this experiment they decided that it was not right for well over a million customers to be buying electricity at a price that subsidized these 17,000 people and therefore increase the price of electricity for the million.

That question of who subsidizes renewables and how much is going to be a political question for a long time to come. I personally think that if society is the one benefitting, then society should pick up the tab. I don't think somebody sitting in a house somewhere in Nevada should be picking up the subsidy for their neighbor. It is not right for 1 million customers in Nevada to subsidize 17,000 customers. The PUC agrees with that. Greg Abel[8] is here. Greg, is there anything you want to add?

**Greg Abel:** As usual, Warren, you've summarized it extremely well. When we think of Nevada it is exactly as you have described it. I'd just add a few things. One, as you've touched on earlier, we absolutely support renewables so we start with the fundamental concept that we are for solar. But, as you highlighted, we want to purchase renewable energy at the market rate – not at a heavily subsidized rate where 1% of the customers will benefit and harm the other 99%. If you take a working family in Nevada who cannot afford the rooftop unit, and you ask them if they want to subsidize their neighbor, the answer is clearly no. At the same time, we are absolutely committed to Nevada, utilizing renewable resources and we are absolutely proud of what our teams are doing. By 2019, we will have eliminated or retired 76% of our coal units and we will be replacing them with solar energy so we are on a great path. We just encourage our team and with the work of the Commission and, obviously, led by the State we'll head down a great path. Thank you.

**Warren:** Put up Slide 7, it will give you a view of what the situation is. This counts all of our Berkshire

---

[8] Greg Abel is Chairman and CEO of Berkshire Hathaway Energy; NV Energy is a subsidiary of BH Energy.

Hathaway Energy operations. In a 20-year period, we will have a 57% reduction [in our coal generation]. You wouldn't want 100% reduction tomorrow. Believe me, the lights would be off all over the country. It's moving at a fast pace.

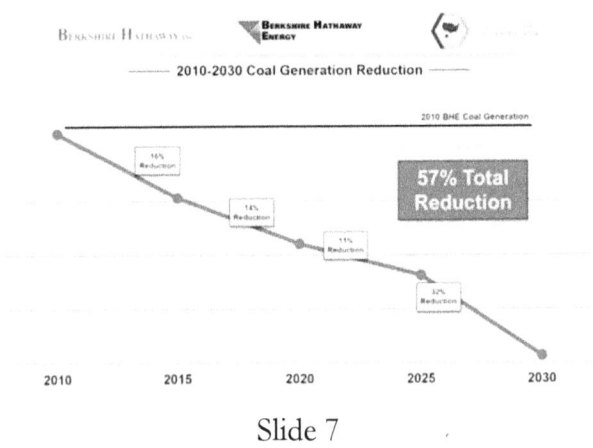

Slide 7

You want to be sure that you treat fairly the people involved in this because somebody pays the cost of electric generation. If you are doing something to benefit the planet, and it's important that it be done, you should not have the costs assessed for that on a specific person who's having trouble making ends meet in their job. Obviously, if you have over a million customers in Nevada a lot of them are struggling and a lot of them are doing fine too. But they are not the ones, in my view, to subsidize the person who can afford to put the solar unit in. Okay, Cliff.

## OIL PRICES

**Q14. Cliff Gallant: Over the past year we've learned, perhaps I've learned that Berkshire's results are more influenced by oil markets than I had previously appreciated. Revenues at the railway company and some of Berkshires manufacturing businesses were negatively impacted and arguably low gas prices hurt GEICO's loss ratio. Yet during this year Berkshire invested in Phillips66, Kinder Morgan and even PCP[9] has revenues associated with the oil and gas industries. I know Berkshire wouldn't make a bet on a commodity like oil but is Berkshire making a statement about the long-term outlook for oil?**

**Warren:** We haven't the faintest idea of what the long-term price of oil is. There's always a better system available. You can buy oil for delivery a year from now or two years from now. We actually did that once. We made money, but we could have made a lot more money. We don't think we can predict commodity prices. We don't hedge cocoa or sugar; I mean we do some forward buying. Basically, we are not two fellows who think that we can predict the price of corn or soybeans or anything else. Anything you have seen in our investment transactions, some of the securities you mentioned were bought by Todd or Ted and one was bought by me, but neither they

---

[9] Precision Castparts Corp., a manufacturer of metal components and products. Berkshire bought it for $37.2 billion in 2015.

nor I bought those, or if we sell them, based on commodity price predictions. We don't know how to do it. We are thinking about other things when we make those decisions. Charlie?

**Charlie:** I'm even more ignorant than you are [about predicting commodity prices].

**Warren:** And that is hard to be.

**Warren:** I think that's the first time I heard him say that. It has a nice ring to it. [laughter] Okay, Station 5.

## STUDENT LOANS AND RISING EDUCATION COSTS

**Q15. Shareholder, Station 5: Hi Warren, Hi Charlie. I'm Ken Martin, I'm an MBA student from the Tuck School at Dartmouth. My question is about college tuition and the problem of rising student debt balances. In the past prominent philanthropists have founded institutions that are now prominent research universities in our country. Why is this not a bigger part of today's philanthropic debate - the founding of new colleges? Would not new supply in higher education be at least part of the solution to this problem?**

**Charlie:** I think if you expect a lot of financial efficiency in American higher education, you are howling at the wind.

**Warren:** He's also saying that more philanthropy ought to be devoted to financing college costs.

**Charlie:** I do a lot more than Warren does in this field and I'm frequently disappointed. Monopoly and bureaucracy are everywhere and universities are not exempt from it. But, of course, they are the glory of civilization. If people want to give more to it, I'm all for it.

**Warren:** You have the option of very good state schools. We spend a lot of money on education in this country. If you take kindergarten through 12, … It's interesting, people talk about entitlements; we talk about entitlements for Social Security and everything. We have entitlements for the young. We spend $600 billion a year educating 50 million kids in the public schools between kindergarten and 12th grade. Nobody ever seems to bring that up. The people in their working ages, generally speaking, in a rich society have an obligation to both the young and the old. Based on the amount we spend, if we have problems with our school system, it's not because we are cheap. There are other problems that contribute to it. In terms of the money we put out, we are right up there. I was a trustee at a college that saw the endowment go from $8 million to over $1 billion. I did not see the tuition come down or the number of students go up.

**Charlie:** Nothing went up except the presidents' salaries.

**Warren:** 8 million to 1 billion and you have very decent people running the place. When you read the figures on endowments at the big schools, some have gotten up to the big numbers. The main objective is to have the endowment grow larger and that will be ever thus. That's the way humans operate. Do you have any more comments on that Charlie, you've seen a lot.

**Charlie:** I've made all the enemies I can afford at the moment.

**Warren:** That's never slowed him down in the past. Andrew?

## DONALD TRUMP

**Q16. Andrew Ross Sorkin: This question is from a shareholder who asked to remain anonymous. If Donald Trump becomes the President of the Unites States and recognizing your public criticism of him and your public support for Hillary Clinton, what specific risks - regulatory policy or otherwise do you foresee for Berkshire Hathaway's portfolio of businesses?**

**Warren:** That won't be the main problem. Government is a very big factor in our business and all businesses. There's the very broad policies that affect practically everybody and sometimes there can be some specific policies. I will predict that if either Donald Trump or Hillary Clinton becomes President, and one of them is very likely to be, I think Berkshire will continue to do fine.

**Charlie:** I'm afraid to get into this area.

**Warren:** We've operated under price controls. We've had 52% federal taxes applied to our earnings for many years and even higher at other times. We've had regulations come along. In the end, business in this country has done extraordinarily well for a couple hundred years. It has adapted to the society, and the society has adapted to business. This is a remarkably attractive place in which to conduct a business.

Imagine in a world of practically zero interest rates, with American business earning terrific returns on tangible equity. Those are the assets that are actually employed in the business. The numbers are staggering. People have had their money in saving accounts that get destroyed but owners of business, if you look at returns on tangible equity they have not suffered even as people that own fixed-investment instruments have suffered enormously. Farmer's income has fallen off in the last few years. Business managed to take care of itself and for a good reason because it contributes to and has been the engine of our market economy that has delivered output that is staggering by the imagination of anyone that might have existed 100 years ago. In my lifetime, the GDP per capita in real terms of the United States has gone up six for one. Can you imagine a society where in one person's lifetime overall, people have six times the real output they had at the beginning? The system works very well in terms of aggregate output. In terms of distribution of that output it can fall very short in my view. It will keep working. You don't have to worry about that. Twenty years from now there will be far more output per capita in the United States in real terms than there is now. In 50 years, it will be far more and the quality will get better. No presidential candidate or President is going to end that. They can shape it in ways that are good or bad, but they can't end it. Now Charlie, give us something pessimistic here to balance me out.

**Charlie:** I want to say something optimistic. I think the GDP figures greatly understate the real advantage that our system has given our citizens. It underweights a lot of huge achievements because they don't translate right into money in a certain way that the economist can easily handle. The real achievements over the last century are way higher than indicated by the GDP figures, and the GDP figures are good. I don't think it's necessarily going to be quite as good as the past, but it doesn't have to be.

**Warren:** There's no one you will run into that says "with my same talents, I wished I lived 50 years ago, born 50 years earlier." A majority of the American public thinks it's a bad time to be born today compared to when they were born. They are wrong. The pace of innovation has never been better – just think how differently you are living. But you're making free choices that were not available to you 20 years ago. I'm still staying with the landline, but you people are way ahead of me. Okay Gregg.

## RAIL MERGERS

**Q17. Gregg Warren:** Warren, late last year we saw Canadian Pacific make a hostile bid for Norfolk Southern, a combination that would have linked Canada's second largest carrier with one of the two largest railroads in the eastern US. This move led to a largely negative reaction from not only Norfolk Southern but from federal and state lawmakers, shippers and other railroad operators even though a formal evaluation process hadn't even begun with the US Service Transportation Board. Canadian Pacific eventually backed down. Looking back to 1999 when the Transportation Board blocked a proposed merger between BNSF and Canadian National, the attitude was that any additional mergers amongst railroads would have to be credited to competition. What do you think they meant by this? And if one believes that the hookup of one of the two major western railroads with one of the two eastern railroads would not alter the current landscape where most shippers have just two choices amongst the large railroads operating in their region and could actually generate efficiencies and cost savings that can be passed along to customers, how does a combination of companies like BNSF and Norfolk Southern or CSX not satisfy their goal?

**Warren:** Matt Rose[10], is he here? He can probably answer some of that better than I can. He can answer all of that better than I can. There is Matt.

**Matt:** Back in 1999, we had a failed merger with Canadian National Railway which was blocked due to new regulations. New rules were put in by a regulator, a little group called the STB.[11] What they said was that the public litmus test for the next merger would have to be different. At that point in time we didn't think a large merger was possible. So when Canadian Pacific announced their merger with Norfolk Southern, when we think of our four constituencies – those four are customers, labor groups, communities in which we serve and the shareholders – we didn't see any interest in the final round of these mergers occurring outside of the shareholder community. Our position was simply to say if the rest of the shipping community believes that we ought to see this final round that's fine, we will participate but we don't see it occurring right now. We do believe that when that final round [of mergers] occurs, there will be great efficiencies made between shippers and communities. Right now, we don't see the dynamics in place. So, what are those dynamics? It will be as the country continues to grow in population from where we are

---

[10] Matthew K. Rose is the Executive Chairman of Burlington Northern Santa Fe (BNSF), http://www.bnsf.com

[11] The Surface Transportation Board (STB) is an independent adjudicatory and economic-regulatory agency charged by Congress with resolving railroad rate and service disputes and reviewing proposed railroad mergers, https://www.stb.gov/stb/about/overview.html

today – 315 million people in the U.S. to 350 million and transportation becomes more scarce [sic], and the railroads will need to do more and that's really when we think the next round will occur.

**Warren:** Okay Station 6.

## INVESTMENT BANKS AND WELLS FARGO

**Q18. Shareholder, Station 6: Hi, my name is Michael Mozzia. I'm from Brooklyn, New York and I'll be starting at Ward Business School in the fall. In an interview with Bloomberg markets recently, Jamie Dimon defended the Royal Bank's playing in financial markets saying banks aren't markets. The market is amoral. You are a trade to the market. A bank is a relationship. But banks, mainly investment banks have struggled as regulators have favored market based solutions and many of those relationships investment banks have worked so hard for have proven to be less lucrative especially compared to the growing fixed costs of supporting them. As it relates to our marketable securities portfolio, how do you feel about the investment banking component particularly as Wells moves into that space? Would you feel differently if the cost basis was higher? And Warren and Charlie, thank you so much for doing this every year.**

**Warren:** Thank you. I didn't totally get that. Is it investment banking firms are being disadvantaged?

**Charlie:** Well, how we feel about what Jamie says that he can't make much money as he used to out of the relationship banking and it's getting tougher and so forth.

**Warren:** Well, the public policy since 2008-09 has been to very much toughen up capital requirements in a variety of ways for banks, but it has specifically been designed to make very large banks less profitable relative to smaller banks. You do that by increasing capital requirements. You can change the math of banking and the attractiveness of banking totally by capital requirements. Obviously, if you said every bank had to have a 100% equity, it would be a terrible business, and you can't possibly earn any money that was significant on capital. If you let people operate with 1% capital ratios, they can make a lot of money, and they will cause the system all kinds of trouble. Since 2009 the rules have been tilted against the larger banks primarily through capital requirements, and that just means returns on equity will go down, but returns on equity were awfully high prior to that. So, it hasn't turned it into a bad business; it's turned it into a less attractive business than earlier. Some of the investment banks operate as bank holding companies and they have been affected by those capital requirements too. I'm not sure if I'm getting 100% of your question, so I'll invite you to give me a follow up if you would like.

**Questioner:** In the marketable securities portfolio, do you feel good about the going forward prospects of the investment banking

**companies especially as Wells Fargo moves into that business?**

**Warren:** Wells Fargo has an investment banking aspect to it that primarily came in through Wachovia[12] but it's not insignificant. Our ownership of Wells Fargo which is very large - it's our largest marketable security – not counting Kraft Heinz which is about the same size. In that situation, we are in the control position. It's the largest non-controlled situation that we have - at Wells Fargo - and that's my intent. I like it extremely well compared to other securities not because it has the most upside.

**Charlie:** It's not the investment banking. It's the general banking of Wells Fargo.

**Warren:** It isn't that big a deal, and that's not what attracts us. We think Wells Fargo is a very well run bank. We didn't make any decision to buy a single share based on the fact that they were going to be more in investment banking business because of the Wachovia acquisition. They've got a lot of sources of income. They've got a huge base of very cheap money but, unfortunately, they've got a lot of very cheap rates on the other side now. We think it's a very well run bank. Investment banking business - Charlie and I are probably a little affected by the experience we have. It's not been something we've

---

[12] Wachovia National Bank was founded on June 16, 1879 in Winston-Salem, N.C. Before acquired by Wells Fargo in 2008, Wachovia was one of the largest diversified financial services companies in the United States.

invested in significantly. We obviously made a major investment in preferred shares of Goldman Sachs. We continue to hold some shares from when we made the investment in 2008. I can't recall us making an investment banking purchase, a marketable security involving an investment bank, for a long time.

**Charlie:** Generally, we fear investment banks more than we love them.

**Warren:** Carol.

## BREAKING UP BERKSHIRE HATHAWAY

**Q19. Carol Loomis: In the conclusion of the book, *Dear Chairman*[13] that you recommend in this year's annual letter, a new book you recommend. The author argues that "the life's work of great investors is inevitably reabsorbed into the industrial complex with little acknowledgement of their accomplishments." He then argues that Berkshire Hathaway will eventually be targeted by activist investors if it trades at too sharp a discount to intrinsic value. Do you agree with this assessment? And have you considered installing corporate defenses that might prevent future generations of activists from trying to break up Berkshire Hathaway?**

---

[13] Dear Chairman: Boardroom Battles and the Rise of Shareholder Activism by Jeff Gramm (HarperCollins, 2016)

**Warren:** I used to worry more about that than I do now. Partly, size is one factor. I think the more important factor is that Berkshire will always be in a position to repurchase very significant amounts of stock. As long as it's willing to buy the stock at some price close to intrinsic value, there should not be a large margin in terms of anybody that might come along and think there'll be a lot of money to be made by breaking up Berkshire. There would be money lost by breaking it up. There will be certain advantages lost. Mid-American Energy could not have done what it has in renewables without Berkshire being the parent. If it had been split off the parts would have been worth less than the whole. I don't think there will be a spread that will be enticing to anyone. Beyond that, the numbers involved would be staggering. I think we have a shareholder base that recognizes the advantages of both the Berkshire businesses and its culture. I think it's very, very unlikely, but there have been periods in business history where stocks sold at dramatic discounts from what you might call intrinsic value. It's interesting that very little activity occurred then. In 1973-1974, there were really good companies, one of which was CapCities [14] that was selling at a huge discount to what it was worth. People did not come along to take advantage of the discount because when discounts are huge, money is usually scarce. It's not a huge worry with me. In my own case, because the way my

[14] Capital Cities Communications was an American media company best known for its surprise purchase of the much larger American Broadcasting Company in 1985. The Walt Disney Company purchased CapCities in 1996.

stock will be distributed after I die, it's very likely that my estate for some years would be by far the largest shareholder of Berkshire in terms of votes. It's not something I worry about now.

**Charlie:** I think we have almost no worries at all on this subject. Other people have justifiable worry, and I think that helps us. I look forward to this subject with optimism.

**Warren:** Do you want to explain how it helps us Charlie?

**Charlie:** If you're being attacked by people you regard as evil [activists], and you want a strong ally, how many people would you pick in preference to Berkshire?

**Warren:** My name is Warren Buffett, and I approve that message. Jonathan.

## LEASING BUSINESS

**Q20. Jonathan Brandt:** Leasing has quietly become an important contributor to Berkshire's earnings with its several leasing units logging about 1 billion in combined annual pretax income. Could you talk about Berkshire's competitive advantages in its various leasing businesses including containers, cranes, furniture, tank cars and rail cars? Are there other leasing businesses you would be interested in entering, for instance, airplanes or commercial

**auto fleets? Plane leasing companies in particular seem to sell for reasonable prices and are often available.**

**Warren:** We've got a very good truck leasing business and extremely very good primarily tank car leasing business. We expanded it by a billion dollars when we bought the GE fleet recently.[15] Leasing generally isn't something – we have to bring something to the party – something extra that's much more than handing people a trailer and taking a check every month. There are important service advantages brought to that. But pure leasing – leasing of new cars, which is a huge business - the math is not that attractive for us. The banks have an advantage because their costs of funds are so low now. It's not quite as low as it looks. But I think Wells Fargo, I think the last figure was down around 10 basis points. When somebody has, you know may be a trillion dollars or so, and then they are paying ten basis points for it, I don't feel very competitive. Berkshire is in that situation. Pure money type leasing is not an attractive business for us when we've got other people with lower cost of funds. I mean they've got the edge. We've got rail car leasing which involves a lot more than a financial transaction. I mean we repair - we got huge activity in the repair field. And those cars require servicing in the same way as in our trailer business. But you will not see us getting into aircraft leasing. That doesn't interest me in the least.

---

[15] Berkshire Hathaway's Marmon Holdings has bought 'substantially all' of GE Railcar Services' tank wagons in 2015.

We've looked at that a lot of times as various aircraft leasing companies offered to us. That's a scary business. Some people have done well in it in recent years by using short-term money to finance longer-term assets which have big residual risks and that isn't for us. Charlie?

**Charlie:** I think you have said it pretty well. We are well located now and I don't think there are huge opportunities in that.

**Warren:** OK, Station 7.

"Valeant, of course, was a sewer and those who created it deserve all the opprobrium that they got."
Charlie Munger

"We have two managers at Berkshire. They each manage $9 billion for us, they both ran hedge funds before. If they had a 2 and 20 arrangement with Berkshire, which is not uncommon in the hedge fund world they would be getting $180 million each, you know, merely for breathing annually."
Warren Buffett

"There's been far, far more money made by people on Wall Street through salesmanship abilities than through investment abilities."
Warren Buffett

# SILVER BULLET

**Q21. Shareholder, Station 7:** Good morning, Warren and Charlie. I am from Vander Marsei from the Philippines. Warren, my wife and I sent original paintings to your office two days ago. We hope you like them.

**Warren:** Thank you.

**Shareholder:** Today Berkshire's size ensures that it faces competition from numerous businesses. If you had a silver bullet, which competitor would you take out and why? And sorry, you can't say Donald Trump.

**Warren:** Which competitor and which businesses?

**Charlie:** Which competitor would you kill if you could? I don't think we have to answer this one.

**Warren:** Charlie is a lawyer. [laughter]. But I have thought about the question. [laughter]. We have lots of tough competitors. In many areas, we are a pretty tough competitor ourselves. What we want our managers to be doing is thinking every day about how to achieve a stronger competitive position; we call it widening the moat. We want better products, we want keep our cost to a minimum, and we want to be thinking about what our customers likely to be wanting from us a month or year or ten years from now. Generally, if you take care of the customer, the customer will take care of you. But there are cases where there is some force coming along that you really may not have the answers for, and then you get out of that business. We had the department store in Baltimore in 1966.[16] And if we kept it, we would have gone out of business. So, recognizing reality is also important. I mean you don't want to try and fix something that is unfixable.

**Charlie:** We aren't targeting competitors for destruction, we are just trying to do the best we can everywhere.

**Warren:** Spoken like an antitrust lawyer. [laughter]. Okay, we really hope to be the ones that the other guy wants to use the silver bullet on it. Becky?

## SEQUOIA FUND AND VALEANT

**Q22. Becky Quick: This question comes from Ron and Rajie Terrakad from Sugarland, Texas. He writes - My wife and I have the vast majority of our net worth invested in Berkshire and in shares of the Sequoia Fund. Mr. Buffett, you have endorsed the Sequoia Fund on more than a few occasions. Recently the Sequoia Fund has been in the news because of its large position in Valeant Pharmaceuticals. Mr. Munger has termed Valeant's Business model as highly immoral. Mr. Buffett, do you agree with Mr.**

---

[16] Warren Buffett invested in Hochschild-Kohn's, a department store chain based in Baltimore, Maryland. Hochschild-Kohn's was founded in 1897. The chain closed in 1983.

**Munger's assessment? Have your views of the Sequoia Fund changed? Also, as you know Sequoia is an admirer and is a large holder of Berkshire stock?**

**Warren:** In a sense, I'm the father of the Sequoia Fund. When I was closing up my partnership at the end of 1969, I was giving back a lot of money to partners. And these people have trust in me and they wanted to know what they should do with their money. We helped out those who wanted to put that into municipal bonds for a few months. Most of them were equity-oriented type investors. And we said there were two people we admired enormously in the investment business, not simply because they were terrific investors but they were terrific people and they would the kind of people you would make trustee of your will. (Those two, one of whom is in the room, Sandy Gottesman, our director). One was Sandy and the other was Bill Ruane. They were friends themselves. Sandy took on a number of our clients or number of our partners. They became clients, and very happy clients of his and I bet some of them are still clients or their children or grandchildren are to this day. A lot of them went with both of them. The majority who had a lot of money gave some to Bill and gave some to Sandy. Bill had a lot of people whose total funds were not of a size that made them economically individual clients. Bill said, "I will set up a fund." They actually had an office in Omaha. John Harding who used to work for me became the employer here. A number of my ex-partners joined Sequoia Fund as a way to find an outstanding investment manager. Like I said - both for ability and for integrity and could deploy small sums with him. Bill ran Sequoia until roughly 2005 when he died, and he did a fantastic job. Even now, if you take the record from inception to now with the troubles they've had recently I don't know if there's a mutual fund in the United States that has a better record – there probably is one or two – but it's far better than the S&P and you won't find records that go for about 30 or 40 years that are better than the S&P. So, Bill did a great job for people. Bill died in 2005. The record continued to be good until a year or so ago. At that time, the management company, or the managers I should say, took an unusually large position in Valeant, despite the objection of some people on the board. They not only maintained that position, but actually increased it after a fair amount of doubt had been expressed by the board about doing that. The record to date still is significantly better than average. My understanding is the manager who made the decision on Valeant is no longer running the operation. Other people will be making an effort to do so and I have every reason to believe. I know that they are very smart decent people who are good, probably way better than the average analyst in terms of Wall Street. I think it was a very unfortunate period when the manager got overly entrenched with the business model. I watched the Senate hearings[17] a couple of days ago when Senator

---

[17] Senate's Special Committee on Aging Hearings on Valeant Pharmaceuticals' Business Model: The Repercussions for Patients and the Health Care System on April 27, 2016, https://www.aging.senate.gov/hearings/valeant-pharmaceuticals-

Collins and Senator McCaskill interrogated three people from Valeant and it was not a pretty picture. In my view, the business model of Valeant was enormously flawed. It had been touted to us, we had several people who urged us strongly to buy Valeant, wanted us to meet persons, that sort of things. But it illustrated a principle that P. Kiewit[18] said many many years ago. He said if you're looking for a manager, find somebody that is intelligent, energetic and has integrity. And he said if they don't have the last be sure they don't have the first two. If they don't have integrity, you want them to be dumb and lazy. If you get an intelligent energetic guy or woman who is pursuing a course of action which you couldn't put on the front page it can make you very unhappy. You can get into a lot of trouble; it may take a while. But Charlie and I have seen – and we are not remotely perfect, I don't mean that – We've seen patterns … you get pattern recognition. It gets very important in evaluating humans and businesses. And pattern recognition is not 100 percent and none of the patterns exactly repeat themselves. There are certain things in business and securities markets that we've seen over and over and frequently come to a bad end but frequently look extremely good in the short run. One which I talked about last year, I'm not referring

business-model-the-repercussions-for-patients-and-the-health-care-system

[18] Peter Kiewit established the construction company, Kiewit Corporation with his brother, Andrew Kiewit in Omaha in 1884. Kiewit is an employee-owned company with a revenue of more than $9 billion in 2015.

to Valeant in this regard, was the chain letter scheme. You're going to see chain letters for the rest of your life. Nobody calls them chain letters these days and that is because that has a connotation that will scare you off. But they are disguised chain letters. Many of the schemes on Wall Street that are designed to fool people have that particular aspect to it. There were patterns at Valeant that I think certainly if you go and watch the Senate hearings, you will see there are patterns that really should have been picked up on. It was very painful to the people of Sequoia. I personally think that the people who are running Sequoia now are able people. I will get into it in a second, the difficulty of managing money. First I will give Charlie a chance to comment on this.

**Charlie:** Well, I totally agree with you that Sequoia has reconstituted – it's a reputable investment fund. If the management is reconstituted, it is a reputable investment advisor. I got quite a few friends and clients that used Ruane Cunniff and I have advised them to stay with the place as reconstituted. And I believe you have done the same. Haven't you?

**Warren:** Right.

**Charlie:** So, we trust the whole thing within is fixed. Valeant, of course, was a sewer and those who created it deserve all the opprobrium that they got. [applause].

**Warren:** In a few minutes, we will break but I think it almost ties in with this last question.

# HEDGE FUND BET

**Warren:** If we could put slide 3 up.

### Protégé Partners Wager Results
### For the Eight Years ended December 31, 2015

| Year | S&P Index Fund | Hedge Funds |
|------|----------------|-------------|
| 2008 | -37.0% | -23.9% |
| 2009 | 26.6% | 15.9% |
| 2010 | 15.1% | 8.5% |
| 2011 | 2.1% | -1.9% |
| 2012 | 16.0% | 6.5% |
| 2013 | 32.3% | 11.8% |
| 2014 | 13.6% | 5.6% |
| 2015 | 1.4% | 1.7% |
| Cumulative | 65.7% | 21.9% |

Some years ago, I made a wager and I promised to report, before the lunch, how the wager was coming out. And I have been doing it regularly but it probably seems appropriate, since it has developed this far, to point out a rather obvious lesson which was what I hoped to drive home to some degree by offering to make the wager originally. Incidentally, when I offered to make the wager, namely, that somebody can pick five hedge funds, and I would take the unmanaged S&P Index used by Vanguard Fund and I would bet that over a ten-year period that the unmanaged index would beat these five funds that were all being managed presumably, (they get to pick any five ones) – that are managed by people who are charging incredibly large sums to people because of their supposed expertise. Fortunately, there is an organization, called or at least you go to the Internet

91

and put in Longbets.org – it's a terribly interesting website – you can have a lot of fun with it. People take the opposite side of various propositions that have a long tail to them and make bets as to the outcome. Each side gives their reasons. You can go to that website (www.longbets.org), and you can find bets about – what population will be doing 15 years from now – all kinds of things. Our bet became quite famous. A fellow I like who I didn't know before this, Ted Seides[19] decided that he could pick out five hedge funds – these are funds of funds. In other words, there was one hedge fund at the top, and that manager picked out who he thought was the best managers underneath and then bought into these other funds in turn – so that five funds of funds represent maybe 100 or 200 hedge funds underneath. Bear in mind that the hedge fund – the fellow making the bet was picking out funds where the manager on top was getting paid perhaps .5% a year, plus a cut of the profits, for merely picking out who he thought were the best managers underneath who were in turn getting paid may be 1.5% to 2% plus a cut of the funds on profits. But, certainly, the guy at the top was incentivized to pick great funds and at the next level those people were presumably incentivized too. The result is after eight years, and several hundred hedge fund managers being involved, the totally unmanaged fund by Vanguard with very very very minimal cost is now 40 some points ahead of the group of the hedge

---

[19] Ted Seides was a founder of Protégé Partners LLC, where he served as President and Co-Chief Investment Officer. He is also the author of the book, *So You Want to Start a Hedge Fund: Lessons for Managers and Allocators* (Wiley, 2016).

funds. Now that might sound like a terrible result for the hedge fund investors, but it's not a terrible result for these hedge fund managers. These managers - you have a top manager charging probably .5% (but I don't know that for sure) and down below you have managers that are probably charging 1.5 to 2%. So, if you have a couple of percentage points sliced off every year, that's a lot of money. We have two managers at Berkshire. They each manage $9 billion for us, they both ran hedge funds before. If they had a 2 and 20 arrangement with Berkshire, which is not uncommon in the hedge fund world they would be getting $180 million each, you know, merely for breathing annually. [laughter]. It's a compensation scheme that's unbelievable to me. That's one reason I made this bet. But what I'd like you to do is for a moment imagine in this room, you people own all of America. All the stocks in America are owned by this group. You are the Berkshire 18,000 or whatever it is that somehow managed to accumulate all the wealth in the country. Let's assume we just divide it down the middle. On this side [pointing to his right-hand side of the auditorium], we put half of all the investment capital in the world. That capital is what a certain presidential candidate might call low energy. In fact, they have no energy at all. They buy half of everything that exists in the investment world - 50% everyone on this side. Now half of it is owned by these no energy people. They don't look at stock prices; they don't turn on business channels; they don't read the Wall Street Journal; they don't do anything. They are a slovenly group that just sits, for year after year after year, owning half of America's business. Now what's their result going to be? The result is going to be exactly average of how American business does because they own half of all of it. They have no expenses, nothing. Now what's going to happen to the other half? The other half are what we call the "hyperactives." Their gross result is also going to be half. Right? The whole has to be the sum of the parts here. This group by definition can't change from its half of the ultimate investment result. This half is going to have the same gross results as the low energy – no energy people. And they are also going to have terrific expenses because they are all going to be moving around, hiring hedge funds, hiring consultants and paying lots of commissions and everything. That half, as a group, has to do worse than this low energy half. The people who don't do anything have to do better than the people that are trying to do better. I mean it's that simple. I hoped, through making this bet, to actually create a little example of that. But that offer was open to anybody. I would make incidentally that same offer now except being around in 10 years to collect that's a little more problematic as we go through life. It seemed so elementary but will guarantee you that no endowment fund, no public pension fund, no extremely rich person wants to sit in that part of the auditorium. They just can't believe that because they have billions of dollars to invest that they can't go out and hire somebody who will do better than average. I hear from them all the time. So, this group over here [pointing to his left hand side] – supposedly sophisticated people, generally richer people – hire consultants. No consultant in the world is going to tell you to just buy an S&P 500 Index fund and sit still for the next 50 years. You don't get to be a consultant that way. You certainly don't get an annual fee that way. So the consultants got every motivation in the world to tell you this year I think we should concentrate more on international stocks; this year, this manager is particularly good on the short side, etc., and so they come in and they talk for hours. You pay them a large fee, and they always suggest something other than just sitting on your rear end and participating in the American business without cost. Then those consultants after they get their fees, they in turn recommend to you other people who will charge fees which, as you can see over a period of time, cumulatively eat up capital like crazy. So, I would suggest that – but I don't feel sure because nothing can tell for sure for any ten-year period – but I certainly thought very probable, otherwise, I would not have struck my neck out. It just demonstrates so dramatically…. I've talked to huge pension funds and taken them through the math and when I leave, they go out and hire a bunch of consultants and pay them a lot of money. It's just unbelievable. The consultants always change the recommendations a little bit from year to year. They can't change them 100% because it would look like they didn't know what they were doing the year before. They tweak them from year to year and they come in and they have lots of charts and PowerPoint presentations. They recommend people who in turn are going to charge them a lot of money and they say well you are going to get the best talent by paying 2 and 20 or something of that sort. The flow of money from the hyperactives to what I call the helpers is dramatic while this group over here sits here and absolutely gets the record of American industries. I hope you realize that for the population as a whole, American business has done wonderfully and the net result of hiring professional management is a huge minus. At the bookstore we have a little book called *Where are the Customers' Yachts?*, written by Fred Schwed. I read it when I was about 10 years old. It had not been updated but new editions have been put up few times. But the basic lessons are there. That lesson is told in that book from 1940. It's so obvious and yet all the commercial push is behind telling you that you are better to think about doing something different today than you did yesterday. You don't have to do that, you just have to sit back and let American industry do its job for you. Charlie, do you have anything to add to my sermon? [applause].

**Charlie:** You're talking to a bunch of people who have solved their problem by buying Berkshire Hathaway and that worked even better. And there have been few of these managers who have actually succeeded. There are few at the universities who are really good. But it's a tiny group of people. It's like looking for a needle in a haystack.

**Warren:** When I was given the job of naming two in 1969 I knew two, well I knew a couple of others. Charlie wasn't interested in managing more money then and my friend Walter Schloss would not scale up well although he had a fabulous record over 45 years or thereabout. But that was all I could come up with at that time. Fortunately, I did have a couple. And the people that went with Sequoia fund have been well served if they stayed for the whole period. There's been far, far more money made by people on Wall Street through salesmanship abilities than through investment abilities. There are a few people out there that are going to have an outstanding investment record but there are very few of them. The people you pay to identify them don't know how to identify them. They do know how to sell to you. That's my message. We will come back at 1 o'clock. Thanks. [applause].

**… Recess …**

# Questions and Answers:
# Part 2

"We are looking for people who are business savvy, shareholder oriented and have a special interest in Berkshire."
Warren Buffett


"… we don't have any committees, but maybe we have some committees that I don't know about, but I've never been invited to any committees, I would put it that way at Berkshire."
Warren Buffett


"We are always behaving a lot like what some might call the Episcopal prayer. We prayerfully thank the Lord that we are not like these other religions who are inferior."
Charlie Munger

**Warren:** Okay, if you will take your seats we will get underway. Next up is Cliff.

## COMMERCIAL INSURANCE

**Q23. Cliff Gallant: Thank you. Berkshire has an online portal for commercial insurance business. I believe its www.coveryourbusiness.com. Is there an opportunity in commercial lines to go direct like what we've seen GEICO do in personal auto insurance?**

**Warren:** The answer to that is we will find out. We have actually two online arrangements. I'm not sure whether they are both up yet. One is called – I believe it's called BIG. I think we got that domain name "BIG" and that will be run by the Applied Underwriters which is a subsidiary of ours that writes workers' comp. The other is run by Ajit. Actually, we do commercial auto – some commercial auto – through GEICO as well. We will learn soon.

(I guess my message about inherited wealth is getting delivered here. [laughter; talking about his latest great grandson mentioned during the intro]. The kid probably wants to put himself for adoption now.)

We have been a little bit and will be experimenting more with various insurance lines. When you look at what has happened with Amazon, you want to try a lot of things. It amazed me how fast the inquiries on personal auto migrated from phone to the Internet, and I would have thought that the younger people would do it, but the people like myself would be very slow to do it. The adaptation by the American public of Internet response has really been pretty incredible and shows no sign of slowing down. The answer is we will try various things and we'll make some mistakes and my guess is 10, 20, 30 years from now it will be a lot different. Station 8.

## SUCCESSION

**Q24. Shareholder, Station 8: Hi, my name is Matt Claybourn from Columbus, Ohio and thank you for putting this on for all of us. My question is: You said before that your role will be divided into parts for your succession. One of which is your responsibility of maintaining culture by having Howard[20] as non-executive Chairman. What is the plan for how Berkshire will maintain its culture when Howard no longer fills the role and what should shareholders watch for to make sure that the culture is being properly maintained decades from now when I am your age?**

**Warren:** That's a question we've obviously given a lot of thought to. Although, I hope that Howard is made chairman just for the reason that if a mistake is made in selecting a successor, it's easier to correct it if you have a non-executive chairman. It may be a 1 in 100 or 1 in 500 probability. There is no sense in ignoring it totally. It's not a key factor. By far, the

---

[20] Howard Buffett, the eldest son of Warren Buffett. He is also the president of Buffett Farms.

main factor in keeping Berkshire's culture is that you have a board, successor board members, managers and successor managers, and you have shareholders that clearly recognize the special nature of the culture. They have embraced the culture when they sold their businesses to us; they wanted to join that culture. It thrusts out people who really aren't in tune with it, and there are very few of them, and it embraces those who enjoy and appreciate it. I think to some extent we don't have a lot of competition on it and so it becomes very identifiable. It works. I think the chances of us going off the rails in terms of culture are really very very slight regardless of whether there's a non-executive chairman or not but that's a small added prediction. I think the main problem that Berkshire will have will be size. I always thought about that when I first started managing money. Size is the enemy of performance to a significant degree. But I do think that the culture of Berkshire adds significantly to the value of the individual components viewed individually. I don't see any evidence that there'll be any board member or any managers or anything that would really move away from what we have now for many, many decades. Charlie?

**Charlie:** I'm even more optimistic than you are.

**Warren:** I've never noticed it.

**Charlie:** I really think the culture is going to surprise everybody by how well it lasts and how well they do.

They'll wonder why they ever made any fuss over us in the first place. It's going to work very well.

**Warren:** We've got so many good ingredients in place in terms of the businesses and the people that are already here. You know that.

**Charlie:** That's what I'm saying. There's just so much power in place.

**Warren:** Another thing that's interesting is how little turnover we get in that too. The number of managers that we've needed to replace in the last ten years is very few. Without a retirement age – and I tend to bring that up at every meeting to reinforce the idea. Without a retirement age and with people being working because they love their jobs - they like the money as well, but their primary motive is they really like accomplishing what they do in their jobs. That means that we get long tenure out of our managers so the turnover is low. The directors are not here for the money. We have great tenure among the directors and I would argue that's a huge plus. It's going to go on a very long time. Andrew.

## DIVERSITY

**Q25. Andrew Ross Sorkin: Thank you Warren. The following question comes from Alex Geldos and several other shareholders asked similar questions that are part of this as well. It's a bit of a multi part question. About two dozen men and women work with you Warren at our corporate**

office. I see from last year the quality of the pictures been improved in the annual report so congratulations on that. However, looking at it there's something that comes to anyone's attention and it is the lack of diversity among the staff. A 2015 analysis by Calvert Investments found that Coca-Cola was one of the best companies for workplace diversity while Berkshire Hathaway was one of the worst. You've explicitly stated that you do not consider diversity when hiring for leadership roles and board members. Does that need to change? Are we missing any investment opportunities as a result? And do you consider diversity, however defined, of company leadership and staff when analyzing the value of a company that you may want to purchase?

**Warren:** Well, it's a multiple part question. The answer to the last question is no. What was the one before?

**Andrew:** You have explicitly said that you do not consider diversity when hiring for leadership roles and board members. Does that need to change? Are we missing any investment opportunities as a result?

**Warren:** We will select board members. We lay it out and have done so for years. I think we've been much more explicit than most companies. We are looking for people who are business savvy, shareholder oriented and have a special interest in Berkshire. We found people like that. As a result, I think we've got the best board that we can have. They are in it - clearly not in it for the money. I get called by consulting firms who've been told to get candidates for directors for other companies. By the questions they ask, it's clear that they've got something other than the three questions we ask in terms of directors in mind. They really want somebody whose name will reflect credit on the institution, which means a big name. You know, one organization recently, the one that did blood samples with small pricks; they got some very big names on their board. Theranos[21] I think. Is that the way you pronounce it, Charlie?

**Charlie:** Theranos, Yah.

**Warren:** I mean the names are great. We are not interested in people that want to be on the board because they want to make $200,000 or $300,000 a year for ten percent of their time, and we are not interested in the ones for whom it's a prestige item or ones that want to go and check boxes or that sort of thing. We will continue to apply that test: business savvy, shareholder oriented, and with a strong personal interest in Berkshire. Every share of Berkshire that our shareholders own, they bought just like everybody else in the room. They haven't got them on auctions. I've been on boards where they have given me stock. I get it for breathing basically – half a dozen places or maybe three or four that I've

---

[21] Theranos is a privately held health technology company based in Palo Alto, California. The previous board included three former secretaries, two senators, one Navy Admiral and one Marine Corps General, https://www.theranos.com

been on the board of. We want our directors to walk in the shoes of shareholders. We want them to care a lot about the business and we want them to be smart enough so that they know enough about business – so know what they should get involved and what they should not get involved in. The people in the office – I'm hoping that when we take the Christmas picture this year, they are exactly the same 25 that we had last year even though we might have added about 30,000 employees elsewhere during the year and maybe $10 billions of sales or something like that. It's a remarkable group of people. I mean just take this meeting, virtually every one of the 25 – our CFO and my assistant, they've been doing job after job connected with making this meeting a success and a pleasant outing for our shareholders. It's a cooperative effort. The idea that you would have some department called annual meeting department and you would have a person in charge of it, and he or she would have assistants and they would go to various conferences about holding annual meetings and then they'd hire consultants to help them…. We just don't operate that way. It's a place where everybody helps each other [applause]. My job is extraordinarily easy, but it's the people around me that really make my job easy. Part of the reason it's easy is because we don't have any committees. Maybe we have some committees that I don't know about. But I've never been invited to any committees, I would put it that way, at Berkshire. We may have a PowerPoint some place. I haven't seen it, and I wouldn't know how to use it anyway. We don't have make work activities. We might go to a baseball game together or something like that. I've seen the other kind of operations, and I like ours better. I would put it that way. Charlie?

**Charlie:** Years ago, I did some work for the Roman Catholic Archbishop of Los Angeles, and my senior partner pompously said, "You know you don't need to hire us to do this. There are plenty of good Catholic tax lawyers." The Archbishop looked at him like he was an idiot and said, "Mr. Pieler, last year I had some very serious surgery, and I did not look around for the leading Catholic surgeon." That's the way I feel about board members. [applause].

**Warren:** Okay, Gregg.

## SHARE REPURCHASES

**Q26. Gregg Warren:** Warren, while Berkshire's authorized share repurchase program originally ended up buying back shares at prices no higher than 10% premium to the firms most recent book value per share, a figure that was subsequently increased to repurchase shares at prices no higher than 20% premium to book value, there has been relatively little share repurchase activity during the last 4 and a half years even as the shares dip down below the 1.2 times book value threshold during both January and February of this year, if you base it on a buy back price calculated on Berkshires book value per share at the end of 2015 – a number that had not yet been published when the stock did dip that low. Given your belief that Berkshire's intrinsic value continues to exceed its book value with the difference continuing to widen over time, are we at a point where it will make sense to consider buying back stock at a higher rate point than Berkshire currently has in place? And would you ever consider stepping in and buying back shares if they did dip down below 1.2 times book value per share even if the prior year's figure had not yet been released?

**Warren:** Gregg, you mentioned that it sold below 1.2. I don't think that's correct. I keep a pretty close eye on that. It's come fairly close to 1.2, but I can almost guarantee you that it hasn't hit 1.2, or we would have done it [repurchased shares]. I will be happy to send you figures on it any day that you might feel that it did hit the 1.2. Clearly, in my view, Charlie's view and the board's, the stock is worth significantly more than 1.2. It should be worth significantly more or we wouldn't have it at that level. On the other hand, we did move it up from 1.1 to 1.2 because we had acquired more businesses over time where the differential between our carrying value and the intrinsic value really had widened from when we set the 1.1. I have mixed emotions on the whole thing. From a strictly financial standpoint, and from the standpoint of the continuing shareholders, I love the idea of buying it at 1.2, which means probably I would love the idea of buying it a little higher than 1.2. On the one hand, it's the surest way of making money per share there is. If you can buy dollar bills for anything less than a dollar, there's no more certain way of making money. On the other hand, I don't enjoy the actual act of buying out people who are my partners at a price that is below – well below what I think the stock is worth. We will buy stocks almost certainly, we don't make it a one hundred percent pledge because there would be a lot of ramifications to that. The odds are extremely high that we would buy a lot of stock at 1.2 times or less, but we would do it in the manner where we are not propping the stock at any given level. If it happens, it will be very good for the stockholders who'll continue. It is kind of an interesting situation though; because if it's true that we will and are eager even, from a financial standpoint, to buy it at that price, it's really like having a savings account where if you take your money out as a dividend or as an interest payment on the savings account, you get a dollar, but if you leave it in, you are almost guaranteed that we will pay you $1.20. Why would anyone want to take money out of a savings account if they could cash it in - what they left - at 120%? So, it acts as a backstop for ensuring that a no-dividend policy results in greater returns than if we paid out a dollar and people got a dollar. If they leave a dollar in, they will get at least $1.20 in my view. It's not a total guarantee, but it's a pretty strong probability. So, would we increase that number? Perhaps. If we run out of ideas, and I don't mean day by day but if it really becomes apparent that we can't use capital effectively within the company in the quantities in which it is being generated, then at some point the threshold might be moved up a little because it could still be attractive to buy it. You don't want to keep accumulating so much money that it burns a hole in your pocket. It's been said actually that a full wallet is little like a full bladder. You may get an urge very quickly to pee it away. We don't want that to happen. So far that hasn't happened. If it ever gets to where we have $100 billion or $120 billion or something like that we might have to increase the price. Anytime you can buy stock back for less than it's worth, it's advantageous to the continuing shareholders. But it should be by a demonstrable margin. Intrinsic value can't be that finely calculated that you can figure it out to four decimal places or anything of the sort. Charlie?

**Charlie:** You will notice elsewhere in corporate America these buyback plans get a life of their own. It's gotten quite common to buy back stock at very high prices. That really don't do shareholders any good at all. I don't know why people are exactly doing it. I think it gets to be fashionable.

**Warren:** It's fashionable, and they get sold on it by advisors.

**Charlie:** Yah, that's true too.

**Warren:** Can you imagine somebody going out and saying we are going to buy a business, and we don't care what the price is? You know we are going to spend 5 billion dollars this year buying a business and we don't care what the price is. That's what companies do when they don't attach some kind of metric to what they are doing on their buybacks.

They say we are going to buy back $5 billion of stock; maybe they don't want to publicize the metric. But certainly, they should say we are going to buyback 5 billion in stock if it's advantageous to buy it back. They say we are going to buy the XYZ Company at this price but we won't buy it at 120% of the price. Jamie Dimon is very explicit about saying he's going to buy back a stock when he's buying it below what he considers intrinsic value to be. I have seen hundreds of buyback notices and I've sat on boards of directors, one after the other, where they voted buybacks, and basically, they said they are doing it to prevent dilution. It has nothing to do with dilution. Dilution by itself is a negative and buying back stock at too high of a price is another negative. It has to be related to valuation. As I say, you will not find a lot of press releases about buy backs that say a word about valuation.

**Charlie:** We are always behaving a lot like what some might call the Episcopal prayer. We prayerfully thank the Lord that we are not like these other religions who are inferior. [laughter]. I'm afraid there's probably too much of that at Berkshire but we can't help it.

**Warren:** Okay, Station 9.

## NEBRASKA FURNITURE MART

**Q27. Shareholder, Station 9: Good afternoon Mr. Buffett. My name is Shawn Montgomery from Fort Worth, Texas. The Nebraska Furniture**

Mart has been opened for about a year in Dallas. I was just curious how sales have been? How they compare to your other stores? And what you think they will be in the future?

**Warren:** It's our largest store in volume, but we had a problem there like we had in Kansas City and that we will probably have every time we open a store. We generated so much initial volume that we had a delivery problem. It was worse in Kansas City. That was the first one we opened. We really had to take our foot off the gas pedal because the last thing we want to do is make first impressions with delivery problems. It's our largest store in volume; the deliveries are getting better – they are actually meeting our company's standards that we have in Omaha but that wasn't the case for some months. We opened up the largest home furniture store in the United States and we did it in an area where we naturally thought we trained the drivers as well as we could. But delivery with 100 plus units out there in the new operation, you know, taking in carpet, people getting lost and routing being bad. There was plenty of work to be done, and it has been done. I expect that store, which already is the largest store we have, to be a billion-dollar annual store before very long. We are getting ready to step on the gas. It's a terrific area. We have 20 plus auto dealerships there in the Dallas/Fort Worth area. We probably have three or four of them in the area where our furniture mart is. They can't build fast enough down there. Toyota is moving there, it already is a great store, but it's going to be something far beyond that. We've opened up about four food places so far and we've got four or five more in the works. They are doing terrific volume. I'm starting to sound like Donald Trump – "Tremendous, terrific, fantastic, I've never seen anything like it!" Just wait until next year. I'll come back, and it will really be in shape then. It's doing well. We could not have picked a better area. We have over 400 acres that we were very fortunate in corralling a whole bunch of land. We are bringing prices and variety like nobody has seen. Now we just have to bring delivery like nobody has ever seen. Okay Carol.

## CNBC – CYBER, NUCLEAR, BIOLOGICAL, AND CHEMICAL THREATS

**Q28. Carol Loomis: This question comes from Chris Gotcho of New York. Mr. Buffett, you have expressed concern about cyber, biological, nuclear and chemical attacks. But preventing catastrophe is not getting enough attention. For example, a bill passed the house unanimously to harden the electric grid against the high altitude nuclear explosion. Not too many bills pass unanimously these days but then the bill got bottled up in the center. Have you considered funding, wouldn't it be a good idea for you to consider funding a lobbying and educational campaign to promote the public good in this area and counteract industry lobbyists who are often more interested in short-term profits?**

**Warren:** Well, in my view, there is no problem remotely like the problem of what I call CNBC – cyber, nuclear, biological, and chemical attacks – that either by rogue organizations, even possibly individuals, or rogue states. You can think about a lot of things. It will happen. I think we have been both lucky, and frankly, the people have done a very good job in government because government is the real protection on this, in not having anything since 1945. We came very very close during the Cuban missile crisis and I don't know what the odds were. I can think of many people that if they had been in place of either Kennedy or Khrushchev, we would have had a very different result. It's the ultimate problem, as I put in the annual report. It's the only real threat to Berkshire – external threat to Berkshire's economic well-being over time. It will happen. I hope when it happens, that it is minimized. The desire of psychotics, and megalomaniacs and religious fanatics and whatever, to do harm to others is a lot more when you have seven billion people on earth than when you had three billion or so which is the case when I was born, less than three billion. Unfortunately, there are means of doing it. If you were a psychotic back far enough you threw a stone at the guy in the next cave. There was sort of a linear relationship of damage to psychosis. I went along through bows and arrows and spears and cannons and various things. In 1945, we unleashed something like the world had never seen. That's a popgun compared to what can be done now. There are plenty of people who would like to cause us huge damage. I came to that view when I was in my 20s and in terms of my philanthropic efforts, I decided that was one of two issues that should be the main issue. I got involved with all kinds of things.

**Charlie:** You supported the Pugwash Conference[22] year after year after year practically all by yourself.

**Warren:** A union of concerned scientists and I've given some money to the nuclear threat initiative that was created – sort of a Federal Reserve System of bank to uranium that will take away some of the excuse for countries to develop their own highly enriched uranium. It's overwhelmingly a governmental problem, and I think it actually has been the top priority for president after president. It's not something they talk about every day and they don't want to scare the hell out of everybody or they also don't want to tip people's hands as to what they are doing, but being in the insurance business (but you don't have to be in the insurance business), you know that someday, somebody will pull off something on a very, very big scale that will be harmful. The United States is probably the most likely place it will happen. It could happen in a lot of other places. That's one huge disadvantage to innovation.

---

[22] Pugwash Conferences for Science and Welfare, which seek a world free of nuclear weapons and other weapons of mass destruction, https://pugwash.org

**Charlie:** Warren, I think he also asked why don't we - Berkshire – spend a lot more time telling the government what they should be doing and thinking.

**Warren:** Well, I've tried telling people. Nobody disagrees on it with you. It seems sort of hopeless to me. They don't know what to do beyond what they are doing. Incidentally, they've done a lot of things. It's not all get publicized. Khrushchev shouldn't have been sending it over to Cuba. At least he had enough sense when he knew Kennedy meant business to turn the ships around. You can't count on there being Kennedys and Krushchevs all the time in charge of things. I see the mistakes that are made in business with human behavior where people act so contrary to their own long range self-interests. There are a lot of frailties. You can argue that if Hitler hadn't been so anti-Semitic, he could have kept a lot of scientists that might have got him to make the Atomic bomb before we did, but he drove out the best of the scientific minds.

**Charlie:** Imagine a guy stupid enough to think the way to improve science is to kick out all of the Jews. [laughter].

**Warren:** The hero of the 20th Century may have been Leo Szilard[23]. Leo is the guy that got Einstein to co-sign a letter to Roosevelt and say, you know, one side

---

[23] Leo Szilard was a Hungarian born physicist and inventory. He was instrumental in getting the United States working on the atomic bomb.

or the other is going to get this, and we better get it first. He said it much more elegantly than that of course, you can go on the Internet and look up the letter. We've both been good and we have been lucky. You remember post 9-11. People started getting a few envelopes with Anthrax and they went to the National Inquirer. When you have a mind that is going to send Anthrax to people, how that decision making is made is just totally beyond comprehension. That person did not end up doing a lot of damage but the capability for damage is absolutely incredible. I don't know how Berkshire does anything about this. I don't know how to do it philanthropically. If I knew how to reduce the probabilities of the CNBC type mass attack by 5%, all of my money would go to that. No question about that, may be 1%.

**Charlie:** Hasn't it been true that we haven't been very good at getting the Government to follow our advice?

**Warren:** But this one is important. [laughter]. Nobody argues with you about it; they just sort of throw up their hands. Some people work for a while on it and just get discouraged and quit. I was involved – I forget the name of it – a bunch of nuclear scientists, that's a long ago. But their idea was to affect elections in small states, the theory being government was the main instrument and you would have the maximum impact. I just went one after another. People took it up and got discouraged. I don't think it's because we've had the wrong leaders. I think our leaders have been good on this. I do not worry about the fact that either Clinton or Trump would regard that as the paramount problem of their presidency. I just don't know that the offense can be ahead of the defense. You can win the game 99.99% of the time but, eventually, anything that has any probability of happening will happen. I wish I could give you a better answer. Charlie, you got any?

**Charlie:** I have no hope of giving a better answer.

**Warren:** That's what they all say to me.

**Warren:** Jonathan.

## LUBRIZOL

**Q29. Jonathan Brandt: The Lubrizol lubricant additives business is one of your six largest non-insurance units but there has been relatively little disclosure about its performance since it was acquired nearly 5 years ago. Can you please update us on how the core business has done and how the competitive landscape and end markets have evolved since it was acquired? I know the core business is not a growth business but has the increase in miles driven helped their top line at all? Could you also talk about the performance of one or two of their more important bolt on acquisitions whether it be Chemtool, Warwick, Weatherfield or Lipotec?**

**Warren:** Yah, the additive business, there are four companies in it basically. It's a no growth but very good business. We are the leader. So, it has performed almost exactly as you would anticipate since purchase; and other specialty companies, some of which might have growth possibilities, but they are small. Lubrizol, overall, on operational basis, has been very much as we anticipated or you would have anticipated if you had looked at the prospectus at the time we bought it. They made one large acquisition which was a big mistake. That was in the oil field specialty chemical area. It was made just about the time or even a little after oil took a nosedive. We have had some decent acquisitions there but the biggest acquisition should not have been made. We still have the fundamental earning power of the additives business and everything. That has not disappointed us in any way, it's a very well run operation that way but It's not a growth operation. Charlie?

**Charlie:** Nothing to add.

**Warren:** OK, Station 10.

## MICROECONOMICS AND MACROECONOMICS

**Q30. Shareholder, Station 10: Hello Mr. Buffett and Mr. Munger. Thank you so much for your insights, teaching and being great role models. My Name is Eric Silberger of New York City. My question for both of you is related to psychological biases. Through Berkshire Hathaway's operations, you get a very good read**

on macroeconomic factors yet Berkshire does not make investment decisions based upon macroeconomic factors. How do you control the effect of information such as knowing microeconomic factors or the anchoring effect of knowing stock prices because after a while it's hard not to once you have analyzed them before? How does that influence your rational decision making whether you should ignore it or whether you should use it in a positive way?

**Warren:** Charlie and I certainly read a lot and we are interested in economic matters and political matters for that matter. So, we know a lot or we are familiar a lot, I should say, with almost all the macroeconomic factors. That doesn't mean we know where we're going to be or where zero interest rates are going to lead. We do know what's going on.

**Charlie:** Warren, there's confusion here. It says microeconomic factors. We pay a lot of attention to those.

**Warren:** Oh yah, I'm sorry. He summed it up.

**Warren:** In terms of the businesses we buy and when we buy stocks, we look at it as buying businesses, so they are very similar decisions. We try to know all or as many as we can know of the microeconomic factors. I like looking at the details of a business whether we buy it or not. I just find it interesting to study the species. That's the way you do study. I don't think there's any lack of interest in those factors or denying the importance of them. Am I getting his question or not Charlie?

**Charlie:** There hardly could be anything more important than the microeconomic factors. That is business. Business and microeconomics is sort of the same term.

Microeconomics is what we do and macroeconomics is what we put up with.

**Questioner: The anchoring effect, how do you deal with that as well?**

**Charlie:** We are not anchored, we are ignoring.

**Warren:** Charlie and I are the kind that literally find it interesting - in every business, we like to look at micro factors. When we buy a See's Candy in 1972, there may have been 140 shops or something. We look at the numbers on each one and watch them over time and we will see third year shops behave over second year shops. We really like understanding businesses. It is interesting to us. Some of the information is very useful. Some of it may look like it's not helpful. But who knows when some little fact stored back of your mind and pops up and may be does make a difference. We are fortunate in that we are doing what we love doing. We love doing this like people like watching baseball games which I like to do too. But the very act - every pitch is interesting, whatever it may be. That's what our activity is and we talk about that sort of thing.

**Charlie:** We try to avoid the worst anchoring effect which is always your previous conclusion. We really try to destroy our previous ideas.

**Warren:** Charlie says if you disagree with somebody, you ought to be able to state their case better than they can.

**Charlie:** Absolutely.

**Warren:** At that point, you've earned the right to disagree with them.

**Charlie:** Otherwise, you should just keep quiet. It would do wonders for our politics if everybody followed my system.

**Warren:** Okay Becky.

"Both of us practically have nothing of significance in the total picture outside of Berkshire. I got some Costco stock because I'm a director."
Charlie Munger

"You've got to be aversive to the standard stupidities. You just keep those out. You don't have to be smart."
Charlie Munger

"You don't need the IQ in the investment business that you need at certain activities in life. But you do have to have emotional control. We've seen very smart people do very stupid things. It's fascinating how humans do that."
Warren Buffett

"Apparently, we've got temperament that has a combination of patience and opportunism in it. And I think it's largely inherited, but it can be learned to some extent."
Charlie Munger

# PERSONAL INVESTMENTS VS BERKSHIRE INVESMENTS

Q31. Becky Quick: Warren, just a quick request, would you please stop using CNBC as an acronym for mass destruction.

Warren: What if I use NBCC, then I've got a problem with Steve.

Becky Quick: This question comes from Matt Bandie in Dallas Texas. He's asking about Seritage Growth Properties. [24] He says in December 2015 you filed a personal 13-G evidencing a roughly 8% ownership position in the real estate investment trust, Seritage Growth Properties which to my knowledge is not paralleled as a Berkshire investment. Alternatively, in September 2015 Warren filed a personal 13-G evidencing ownership in Phillips66 which is paralleled as a Berkshire investment. My question is how do you decide when making a personal investment for your own account versus an investment for Berkshire? I understand market cap and ownership sizing are the likely factors but does it still not behoove him to invest

---

[24] Sears (NASDAQ: SHLD) sold 235 store properties and its interest in another 31 properties to a newly formed real estate investment trust (REIT) called Seritage Growth Properties (NYSE: SRG) for $2.7 billion in 2015. The deal gave Seritage control of some of Sears' best properties in a sale-leaseback transaction. ESL Investments owns 43.5% of the limited partnership units of Seritage and 7.9% of the REIT's voting power.

for the shareholders' benefit in a company like Seritage that might have significant upside and where are you putting your personal money to work?

**Warren:** Right. I do not own a share or never have owned a share of Phillips66. I'm not sure where that person is referring to. Maybe there's some way when the form is filled out that because I'm CEO of Berkshire, on some line, it imputes ownership to me or something. The answer is I've never owned a share of Phillips. Seritage is a real estate investment trust that had a total market value of under $2 billion when I bought it. My situation is that I have about 1% of my net worth outside of Berkshire and 99% in it. I can't be doing things that Berkshire does. Seritage with a 2 billion market cap is not something of Berkshire size, and we've never owned a real estate investment trust to my knowledge or my memory in Berkshire at all. I could buy that and not have any worry about a conflict with Berkshire. As a practical matter, my best ideas – I hope they are my best ideas - are off limits for me because they go to Berkshire if they are sizable enough. They will have a significance to Berkshire. We will not be making investments, (unless it's something very odd) we will not be making investments in companies with a total market cap of a couple of billion. So, every now and then, I see something that is sub-sized for Berkshire that I will put that 1% of my own net worth in and the rest of the stuff is off limits basically unless Berkshire is all done buying something. I own some Wells that I bought a long, long time ago. Berkshire was not interested – we bought enough or we didn't have enough money. I try to stay away from anything that could conflict with Berkshire and if I'd been buying Phillips when Berkshire was buying Phillips or prior or subsequently, there could be a case where it would be okay where we might get something. But the answer is I didn't buy any and I never owned any. Charlie?

**Charlie:** Well, part of being in a position like that is you really don't want a conflict of interest or even the appearance of it. And it's been fifty or sixty years when we embarrass Berkshire by side trading. Both of us practically have nothing of significance in the total picture outside of Berkshire. I got some Costco stock because I'm a director. Berkshire has some Costco stock. There are two or three little overlaps like that, but basically Berkshire shareholders have more to worry about than some conflict Warren and I are going to give it. We are not going to do it.

**Warren:** It may sound a little crazy, and it's only because I can afford to say this, but I would much rather make money for Berkshire than for myself. It's not going to make any difference to me anyway. I have all the money I can possibly need and way more. I am balanced; my personality and everything is more wound up in how Berkshire does than I am myself because I'm going to give it all away. I know my end result is going to be zero, and I don't want Berkshire's end result to be zero. I'm on Berkshire's side. Cliff. [applause]

# FREE CASH FLOW

**Q32. Cliff Gallant: One of the great financial characteristics of Berkshire today is its awesome cash flow. While a simple earnings less CAPEX formula yields an annual free cash flow calculation of I figure around $10 to $12 billion. In reality, it seems to be much higher, closer to $20 billion and I think in part due to changes and the deferred taxes year to year. What is the outlook for free cash flow and can investors continue to expect similar dynamics going forward?**

**Warren:** There's a lot of deferred tax that is attributable to unrealized appreciation of securities. I don't have the figure, but let's just assume it's $60 billions of unrealized appreciation of securities. Well, then there would be $21 billions of deferred taxes. That isn't really cash that's available; it's just an absence of cash that's going to be paid out until we sell the securities. Some arises through bonus depreciation. The railroad will have depreciation for tax purposes that's a fair amount higher than for book purposes. Overall, I think of primarily the cash flow of Berkshire as a practical matter relating to our net income plus our increase in float, assuming we have an increase. And over the years, float has added $80 billion plus to make available for investment beyond what our earnings allowed for. That's a huge element. We are going to spend more than our depreciation in our businesses – the railroad and Berkshire Hathaway Energy are two entities that will spend quite a bit more than depreciation in all likelihood – for a long, long time. The other businesses, unless we get into inflationary conditions, it won't be a huge swing one way or the other. So, our earnings, not counting capital gains, of around $17 billion, plus our change in float is the net new available cash. But, of course, we can always sell securities and create additional cash or we can borrow money and create additional cash. It's not a very complicated economic equation at Berkshire. People for a long time didn't appreciate the value of float; we kept explaining it to them and I think that they probably do now. The big thing, the goal, what Charlie and I think about, we want to add every year something to the normalized earning power per share of the company. We think we can do it because we should be able to do it and we have retained earnings to work with every year to get that job done. Sometimes it doesn't look like we have accomplished much and we haven't accomplished much and in other years something big happens. We don't know ahead of time which year is going to be which. Charlie?

**Charlie:** There are very few companies that have ever been similarly advantaged. In the whole history of Berkshire Hathaway, we lived with a torrent of money and we were constantly deploying it and dispersed assets and we were rising up as we went along. That's a pretty good system. We are not going to change it.

**Warren:** It's allowed for a lot of mistakes. That's the interesting thing. American business has been good enough that you don't have to really be smart to get a decent result. If you can bring a little bit of intellect, you should get a pretty good result.

**Charlie:** What you've got to do is be aversive to the standard stupidities. You just keep those out. You don't have to be smart.

**Warren:** Thank God.

Charlie: Thank God, right.

**Warren:** Okay Station 11.

## THINKING AHEAD OF THE CROWD

**Q33. Shareholder, Station 11: Hey Warren and Charlie. Thank you so much for your generosity and sharing your life's accumulation of knowledge and financial capital to the progress of humanity, thank you for that. Berkshire managers thank you for building important companies and stewarding our financial futures, thank you guys. This is Bruce Wang from Micro Jig, traveling west from Orlando, Florida. Last year you kindly shared with me the importance of getting the best reputation you can and behaving well. This year I'd like to ask in preface with the Bill Gates wrote. "Warren's gift is being able to think ahead of the crowd. It requires more than taking his aphorisms to heart to**

accomplish that, although **Warren** is full of aphorisms well worth taking to heart." And he also added that "I've never met anyone who thought in business in such a clear way." Warren, what elusive, yet obvious to you, truth has allowed you to think ahead of the crowd and build a clear mental framework to produce a historically significant institution powerhouse brand? And Charlie same to you what obvious truth presents itself so clearly to you but many would fervently disagree with you upon?

**Warren:** I think I got the question. I owe a great deal to Ben Graham in terms of learning about investing, and I owe a great deal to Charlie in terms of learning a lot about business. I spent a lifetime looking at businesses and why some work and why some don't work. As Yogi Berra said, "You can see a lot just by observing." That's pretty much what Charlie and I have been doing for a long time. I mentioned pattern recognition earlier. I would say it's important to recognize what you can't do. We may have tried the department store business and a few things, but we've generally tried only to swing at things in the strike zone, in our particular strike zone. It's really has not been much more complicated than that. You don't need the IQ in the investment business that you need at certain activities in life. But you do have to have emotional control. We've seen very smart people do very stupid things. It's fascinating how humans do that. Just take the people that get very rich and then leverage themselves in some way that then lose everything. They are risking something

135

that's important to them for something that isn't important to them. You can figure that one out in first grade but people do it time after time. You see that constantly, that self-destructive behavior of one sort or another. It doesn't take a genius to do it, but we have sort of avoided the self-destructive behavior. Charlie?

**Charlie:** Well, there are a few simple tricks that work well. Apparently, we've got the temperament that has a combination of patience and opportunism in it. And I think that's largely inherited, although it can be learned to some extent. Then I think another factor that accounts for the fact as to why Berkshire has done so well is that we are really trying to behave well. I had a great-grandfather that when he died, the preacher gave the talk and said, "None envy this man's success so fairly won and wisely used." That's a very simple idea but it's exactly what Berkshire is trying to do. There are a lot of people that made a lot of money, and everybody hates them. They don't admire the way they earned the money. I'm not particularly admirable of making money running gambling casinos and you know we don't own any. We've turned down businesses, including a big tobacco business. So, I don't think Berkshire would work as well if it were just terribly shrewd but didn't have a little bit of what the preacher said about my grandfather. We want to have people think of us as having won fairly and used wisely. It works. [applause].

**Warren:** We were very very lucky to be born when we were and where we were. You could have dropped us at some other place in time or some other part of the world and things would have turned out differently.

**Charlie:** Think of how lucky you were to have your Uncle Fred. Warren had one uncle, one of the finest men I ever knew. I used to work for him, too. A lot of people have terrible relatives. [laughter].

**Warren:** Just yesterday we had a meeting of all my cousins and a whole bunch that we just get together around the annual meeting time. There were probably 40 or 50 of us there. They were pulling out some old pictures. I had four aunts, they are all in these pictures. Every one of them - you were so lucky to have just one like that, and I had four! In every way, they reinforced a lot of things that needed some reinforcement in my case.

**Charlie:** I wish you had a couple more. We'd be doing even better.

**Warren:** He [Charlie] mentioned my uncle Fred but my aunt Katie worked in the store too and my aunt Alice worked in the store. You just couldn't have been around better people. I think Charlie would agree with that.

**Charlie:** Yeah, we were very lucky.

**Warren:** My grandfather was a little however. Tell them what my grandfather used to do when he paid you [Charlie] on Saturday.

**Charlie:** Well that was very interesting, Warren is a Democrat. But he came from different ancestries. I worked for his grandfather, Ernest, and he was earnest. When they passed Social Security which he disapproved of, because he thought it would reduce self-reliance. He paid me $2 for ten hours work. There was no minimum wage in those days on Saturday and it was a hard 10 hours. At the end of the ten hours, I came in and he made me give him 2 pennies which was my contribution to Social Security and then he gave me two one dollar bills and a long lecture on the evils of Democrats, the welfare states and the lack of self-reliance and went on and on and on. I had Ernest Buffett telling me what to do.

**Warren:** Okay enough family history.

**Charlie:** I haven't overstated that, have I ever?

**Warren:** You haven't overstated that at all.

**Charlie:** You can't believe that people. And he thought he was doing his duty to the world by doing that.

**Warren:** But we were lucky - the people we were around when we were young. We were very lucky. Andrew.

# DUE DILIGENCE ON DEALS

**Q34. Andrew Ross Sorkin:** Warren and Charlie, you are famous for making a deal over a day or two with nothing more than a handshake. You pride yourself on the small overhead of doing the diligence mostly yourself. Other successful acquisitive companies use teams of internal people, outside bankers, consultants and lawyers to do due diligence often over many months to assess deals. Speed may be a competitive advantage; you have done some amazing deals. But does your diligence process also put us at greater risk? And if you're ever gone how would you recommend Berkshire change how we approach deal making?

**Warren:** I get that question fairly often, often from lawyers. In fact, we talked to Munger, Tolles, the law firm and that was one of the questions I got: why we didn't do more due diligence — which we would have paid them by the hour for. It's interesting. We've made plenty of mistakes in acquisitions and also mistakes in not making acquisitions. The mistakes are always about making an improper assessment of the economic conditions in the future of the industry or the company. They are not a bad lease, they are not a specific labor contract, they are not a questionable pattern. They are not the things that are on the checklist for every acquisition by every major corporation in America. Those are not the things that count. What counts is whether you're wrong about what you are really going to fix on the basic economics and how the industry is likely to develop or whether Amazon is likely to kill them in a few years, that sort of thing. We've not found a due diligence list that gets at what we think are the real risks when we buy a business. We have certainly made at least half a dozen mistakes and maybe more when you talk about mistakes of omission. But none of those could have been cured by a lot more due diligence; they might have been cured by us being a little smarter. It just isn't the things that are on the checklist that really count. Assessing whether a manager who I'm going to hand a billion dollars to for his business and he is going to hand me a stock certificate, assessing whether he's going to behave differently in the future in running that business than he has in the past when he owned it, that's incredibly important. There's no checklist in the world that's going to answer that. So, if we thought there were items of due diligence — there are a few that get covered, (you want to make sure that they don't have twice as many shares out as you're buying), that sort of thing. But if we thought there were things that were missing that were important in assessing the future economic prospects of the business, we would by all means drill down on those. When we bought See's, we probably had 150 leases. When we buy Precision Castparts, there are 170 plants. There will be pollution problems at some place. That does not determine whether a 32 billion dollar acquisition is going to look good five or ten years from now. We try to focus on those things. I do think it probably facilitates things with at least certain people, that our method of operation does cut down [the cost of due diligence]. In some acquisitions, you find people get into squabbles on small things – I've seen deals fall apart because people start arguing about some unimportant point. Their egos get involved, they draw lines in the sand, and all of that. I think we gain a lot. When we start to make a deal, it usually gets done. Charlie?

**Charlie:** You started to think about it, business quality usually counts for something more than whether you crossed the t's on some old lease or something. The human quality of the management who are going to stay are very important and how are you going to check that with due diligence? I don't know anyone who has had a generally better record than Berkshire in judging business quality and the human quality of people who are going to lead the business. I don't think it would have improved at all by using some different method. I think that the answer for us at least is we are doing it the way we should.

**Warren:** Negotiations that drag out have a tendency to be more likely to blow up for some reason. People can get obstinate about very small points. And it's silly to get obstinate, but people get silly sometimes. I like to keep things moving, and I like to show a certain amount of trust in the other person because usually trust comes back to you. You know, the truth is there are some bad apples out there and spotting them is not going to come from looking at some documents. You really have to size up whether that person who is getting a lot of cash from you, how they are going to behave in the future because we are counting on them. That assessment is as important as anything involved. We know all the figures going in and we know what we will pay. We don't want things to get gummed up in negotiation. I am perfectly willing to lose small points here and then if I have the deal on the right terms. Tom Murphy taught me this: you just don't try to win every point. It's a terrible mistake. You make a decent deal if you find something that can be done or delivered some way that's Okay. If you think it's bad faith and it gives an indication of the character of the person you're dealing with, then you've got another problem. You're lucky if you find that out early. Charlie anymore?

**Charlie:** How many people in this room who are happily married carefully checked their spouse's birth certificate and so on? My guess is that our methods are not so uncommon as they appear.

**Warren:** I'll think about that. Okay, Gregg.

## SUCCESSION PLANNING

**Q35. Gregg Warren: Warren, the announcement earlier this month that Ajit Jain would be taking over responsibility for all of Berkshire's reinsurance efforts once Tad Montross retires from General Re has raised some questions about not only the change in leadership structure but succession planning. Given the state of the reinsurance market, it makes sense to have Ajit**

overseeing both businesses, especially if the pricing environment is expected to be difficult for another 10 years. There are duplicate of efforts that can be streamlined. Given this move and the change in responsibilities we've seen at several of Berkshires subsidiaries in the last few years, I was just wondering if you could give us some color on how succession planning is handled at the subsidiary level. Any insight you can give us into what led you to finally decide to have Ajit oversee both of Berkshire's reinsurance arms and whether or not it will change the amount of work he will be doing on the specialty side of the business would be greatly appreciated.

**Warren:** Tad Montross after 39 years has done an absolutely sensational job for Berkshire. [applause]. Gen Re was a problem child for a while as you know, some brought on by itself and some external. Tad is sensational and I tried several times, maybe successful in terms of months but not years to get him to stay on longer. As you say, it makes sense to have the reinsurance operation under Ajit. Ajit's ability to handle more and more things in insurance, he oversees a company called Guard[25] which most of you have never heard of. We bought it a few years ago and it's doing terrifically. It is based in Wilkes-Barre, PA. It's doing a great job with small business

---

[25] A national insurer which provides commercial property and casualty insurance, workers' compensation coverage, commercial umbrella, commercial auto, and disability policies in a rapidly expanding number of select states, https://www.guard.com

policies primarily workers comp around the country and it's flourished under Ajit. He started the specialty operation a couple years ago under Peter and that's going gangbusters. I have found, and this is interesting but it's true, with really abled people, they can handle so much. Just take Carrie Sova who put this meeting together. You know if you have some preconceived notion, that for an annual meeting that's going to have 40,000 people, you'll need to spend millions of dollars with all kinds of organizational planning, meetings and meetings, ... but really abled people, ... like my assistant Debbie Bosanek, she can do anything. There's just no limit to what talented people can accomplish. If I had something else in insurance tomorrow that needed doing, I'd probably call Ajit on that too. In terms of my succession, that's something ... we will have a board meeting on Monday ... and we will talk about it as we always do at every meeting. Our thoughts are as one on that, and everybody knows why it makes the most sense. Five years from now, something else could make sense and that's one reason for not announcing any names now. Who knows what might happen in terms of the time when it happens or what happens to the person involved? Maybe their situation changes. There are no tea leaves to read in the fact that Ajit is supervising Gen Re from this point forward. Charlie?

**Charlie:** Well, there is an upper side of that. Not only can the abled people usually do a lot more, but the unabled people by and large you can't fix. You are forced to use our system if you have your wits about you.

**Warren:** We don't feel the need to follow any kind of organizational common view as to – you do this and you have only so many people that can report to you, that sort of thinking. At Berkshire, with every decision comes up, we just try and figure out the most logical thing to do at that time. We don't have a grand design in mind, like an Army organizational chart or something of the sort, and we never will.

**Charlie:** Warren and I once reached a decision that we wouldn't pay more than X dollars for some things. A man who was subordinate to both of us, who is an archeologist said "You guys are out of your minds. This is really stupid. This is a quality operation. You ought to pay up for it." We just looked at one another and did it his way. We don't pay any attention to titles.

**Warren:** He was right too.

**Charlie:** He was right. Of course.

**Charlie:** A chair woman gave us a good idea that we will accept for chair folding.

**Warren:** Actually, one time the woman that does clean my office came in. She was kind of wondering what I did. I have seen her frequently. Her name was Ruby. Finally, one day she decided to get to the heart of the matter. She said, "Mr. Buffett, do you ever get any good horses?" That's apparently where she thought I was getting my money, at the track. [laughing] Okay, Station 1.

## BERKSHIRE'S CREDIT RATING

**Q36. Shareholder, Station 1: Hello Mr. Buffett, Mr. Munger. I'm from Massachusetts. Thank you for taking my question. With Berkshire Hathaway being so well managed why doesn't it have a highest credit bond rating?**

**Charlie:** Let me take that one, the rating agencies are wrong [applause] and set in their ways.

**Warren:** And we don't fit their model very well. We don't look like anything exactly they see otherwise.

**Charlie:** That's the answer.

**Warren:** When they come in the door, I always say let's talk quadruple A. I believe in starting the negotiation from that standpoint. I never get any place. Okay Carol.

## 3G AND COST CUTTING

**Q37. Carol Loomis: Questions continue to come in about the financing and working relationship that Berkshire formed with 3G a couple of years ago and this is one of those questions. While 3G has been very successful in cutting costs, and increasing margins at Kraft Heinz, the company**

has seen volumes and revenues decline. As a long-term investor, how do you judge when a management is cutting muscle as well as fat? Can a business increase revenues while cutting costs? And I forgot to say this came from Rick Smith at New York City.

**Warren:** Well the answer is yes, that sometimes you can cut costs that are a mistake to cut and sometimes you can keep costs that are a mistake to keep. Tom Murphy had the best approach. He never hired a person he didn't need, and therefore, he never had layoffs. You might say that at headquarters at Berkshire we follow a similar approach. We just don't take on anybody. Now if you're in a cyclical business, you may have to cut your work force because there aren't as many car loads of freight moving or something like that. So, you cut back on train crews and all that. But I think it is totally crazy - the idea that you give up your staff or whatever, maybe economists, or something like that because business has gone down. If you don't need them now then you didn't need them in the first place. People that are there just because somebody started a department and they hired more people and so on, I would argue that since we've forgotten to insult this group so far, I would suggest that that happens in investor relations departments perhaps or something of the sort. You get a department going and they always going to want to expand. The ideal method is not to do it in the first place. But there are all kinds of American companies that are loaded with people that aren't doing anything or are doing the wrong thing. If you cut that out it should not really have any significant effect on volume. On the other hand, if you cut out the wrong things you could have a big effect. It can be done in a dumb way or a smart way. My impression from everything I've seen, and I've seen a fair amount so far, is that 3G in terms of the cost cuts that they have made have been extremely intelligent about it and have not done things that will cut volume. It is true in the packaged good industry, volume trends for everybody whether they are fat or lean in their operation. Volume trends are not good. The test will be over time – 3 to 5 years - are the operations which have had their costs cut, do they do poorly in terms of volume than the ones that in my judgment look very fat? So far, I see no evidence of that whatsoever. I do think at Kraft Heinz for example, we've got certain lines that will decline in volume and we've got certain lines which will increase in volume. Overall, the packaged goods industry is not going to go anyplace in terms of physical volume and it may decline just a bit. I have never seen anybody run anything more sensibly than 3G has in terms of taking over operations where costs were unnecessarily high and getting those costs under control in a hurry. The volume question, we will look at as we go along. Believe me, I look at those figures every month and I look at everybody else's figures every month. I'm always looking for any signs of underperformance because of any decisions made. And I've seen none. Charlie?

**Charlie:** Sometimes when you reduce volume, it's very intelligent because you are losing money on the volume you're discarding. It's quite common for a business not only to have more employees than it needs, but sometimes is has two or three customers that you would be better off without. So, it's hard to judge from the outside whether things are going good or bad just because volume is going up or down a little. Generally speaking, I think the leanly-staffed companies do better at everything than the ones that are overstaffed. I think overstaffing is like getting to weigh 400 pounds when you're a normal person. It's not a plus.

**Warren:** Sloppy thinking in one area probably indicates there may well be sloppy thinking elsewhere. I have been a director of 19 public corporations and I've seen some very sloppy operations and I have seen a few really outstanding business operators. There is a huge difference. If you have a wonderful business, you can get away with being sloppy. We could be wasting a billion dollars a year at Berkshire, $650 million after tax, that would be four percent of earnings, and maybe you wouldn't notice it. But …

**Charlie (interjecting):** I would. [laughter].

**Warren:** It grows. Yes, Charlie would notice it. It's the really prosperous companies – the classic case were the tobacco companies many years ago – they went off into this thing and that thing, and it was practically play money because it was so easy to make. It didn't require good management, and they took advantage of that fact. You can read about some of that in *Barbarians at the Gate*.[26] Okay, Jonathan.

## VAN TUYL ACQUISITION

**Q38. Jonathan Brandt: Berkshire paid 4.1 billion for Van Tuyl's Auto retailing business and consolidated its earnings for nearly 10 months last year. Given prevailing acquisition multiples in the industry and margins and the record level of retail auto sales it seems that the acquisition should have contributed more to Berkshire's bottom line in 2015 than it seemed to. Although it's hard to tell for sure since it's results were lumped in with those of the German motorcycle apparel acquisition which was only owned for a part of the year also. I understand the tax deductible and tangibles reduce the effective purchase price of Van Tuyl but I still wonder whether there were any one-time charges or whether profits from insurance and finance operations could have been reported somewhere other than in the retail segment. I imagine Berkshire is earning a better return on the acquisition than is so far apparent but I wonder if you could explain the difference between the likely economics of the deal and what I infer from the annual report figures.**

---

[26] *Barbarians at the Gate: The Fall of RJR Nabisco* by Bryan Burrough and John Helyar (Harper & Row, 1989). Also available as a movie.

**Warren:** Well, you are right about it. It's better than it looks. For one thing, we got a billion dollars of securities roughly with the $4.1 billon. Those securities were basically carrying at a quarter of one percent. That billion is available to us and that came with the deal. There's some very significant acquisition accounting charges that will continue for a couple years and that I'm happy to have taken that way. The economics of Van Tuyl, I would say, have worked out almost exactly. If you had asked me a year ago to lay out a projection, I don't do that. But if I had, it would look very much like things have turned out. And Jeff Rachor who runs that operation really fits the Berkshire mold. We've got a first-class CEO there. But take a billion dollars off the purchase price for openers and then there are some amortization charges of items that are allowable that make you correctly see a fairly low figure against what it appears the acquisition price was. So far, it's exactly on schedule and the schedule was perfectly satisfactory. Okay, Station 2.

Incidentally, we haven't had much luck so far in acquiring other auto dealerships based on the same metrics that we bought Van Tuyl and I think, to a small degree, that's because people think we paid more for Van Tuyl than we did. They aren't seeing certain factors and so they think we paid X. Therefore, they think they are entitled to X. But we didn't pay X. We bought very little so far and I hope that changes in the future. We are not going to change our metrics in terms of how we value auto dealerships. Okay Station 2.

# ZERO AND NEGATIVE INTEREST RATES

**Q39. Shareholder, Station 2:** Good afternoon Mr. Buffett and Mr. Munger. I am John Gory from Iowa City, Iowa. When interest rates go from zero to a negative in a country, how does that change the way that you value a company or a stock? Do you choose a high valuation because the discount rate is low? Or on the other hand do you choose a low valuation because the cash flow is likely to be poor?

**Warren:** Well going from, (which we haven't done that in this country yet), going from 0% to - ½%, is really no different than going from 4% to 3 ½%. It has a different feel to it obviously, if you have to pay a half a point to somebody. If you have your yield or your base rate reduced by a ½% point, it's of some significance, but it's not dramatic. What's dramatic is interest rates being where they are generally - whether it's 0, plus a quarter, minus a quarter, plus a half, minus a half - we are dealing with the situation essentially very close to 0 interest rates and we have been for a long time and longer than I would have anticipated. The nature of it is that you will pay more for a business when interest rates are zero than when they are 15% when Volcker was around and you can take that up and down the line. We don't get too exact about it because it isn't that exact a science. But very cheap money makes me pay a little more for businesses than when money was what we previously thought were very normal interest rates, and very tight money would cause me to pay somewhat less.

We had a rule for 2600 years that Aesop lived around 600 BC. He didn't know that it was BC (but you cannot know everything). And it was that a bird in the hand is worth two in the bush. A bird in the hand now is worth about 9/10th of a bird in the bush in Europe. Well it depends on how far the bush is, it keeps getting worth less the further it goes on. These are very unusual times that way. If you asked me whether I paid a little more for Precision Castparts because interest rates are around zero than if they had been 6%, then the answer is yes. I try not to pay too much more, but it has an effect. If interest rates continue at this rate for a long time, if people ever really start thinking something close to this is normal that will have an enormous effect on asset values. It already has some affect. Charlie?

**Charlie:** I don't think anybody really knows much about negative interest rates. We never had them before. We never had periods of stasis, except for the Great Depression. We didn't have things like what happened in Japan, great modern nation playing all monetary tricks, Keynesian tricks, stimulus tricks, mired in stasis for 25 years. None of the great economists who studied this and taught it to our children understand it either. We just do the best that we can.

**Warren:** They still don't understand it.

**Charlie:** No. Our advantage is that we know we don't understand it.

**Warren:** It's interesting though. It makes for an interesting movie. It does modestly affect what we pay for businesses – I don't think anyone expected it to last this long, do you Charlie? Personally?

**Charlie:** If you are not confused, you haven't thought about it correctly.

**Warren:** I've thought about it correctly then. Becky.

"The basic rule of incentives is you get what you're rewarded for. If you have a dumb incentive system, you get dumb outcomes."
Charlie Munger

"If you were a consultant [compensation consultant], you would want to make people think that it is very complicated and that only you can solve this terrible problem for them that they can't solve."
Warren Buffett

"There's something to be said for leaning over backward to have a win-win relationship with both suppliers and customers, always."
Charlie Munger

"Let me take that one. That's a question like asking, "Why don't you kill your mother to get the insurance money?" We don't do it."
Charlie Munger

# IBM AND GEICO RELATIONSHIP

**Q40. Becky Quick:** Warren, in the past you've talked about **GEICO** working with **IBM's** Watson and this shareholder, Guillaume Bromudaz, writes in and wants to know: Would **IBM** be able to offer insurance industry competitors of **GEICO** the solutions developed with **GEICO's** help and expense? I would think that there would be confidentiality provisions to protect **GEICO** because in as much as **GEICO** educates **IBM** as to insurance issues, **GEICO** could be at jeopardy of competitors gaining or equaling its advantage if they purchase solutions jointly developed by **GEICO** and **IBM.**

**Warren:** I would say that the answer to that if both parties thought about that matter, very intensively and extensively, neither would be in a position to talk about it. I don't like to not answer any questions, but there are some things it doesn't pay to answer. Am I right, Charlie?

**Charlie:** Of course, you're right.

**Warren:** I like that. Cliff.

# AMERICAN EXPRESS

**Q41: Cliff Gallant:** You have long stressed the importance of taking a long-term view when investing. Over the decades your substantial returns on American Express seemed to support your point. **You have talked in the past about the ability of American Express to reinvent itself over time but today it seems to be a company that doesn't have alternative businesses and its brand doesn't seem to have the same cachet as it once did. Shouldn't a prudent investor, shouldn't Berkshire periodically reassess its reasons for owning an investment?**

**Warren:** We reassess our reasons for owning all investments on an almost continuing basis. Both Charlie and I do that. Usually we are in a general range of agreement, but sometimes we are a fair distance apart perhaps. There is no question that payments are an area of intense interest to a lot of very smart people who got a lot of resources and [clearing throat].

**Charlie:** And rapid change.

**Warren:** Yah and rapid change and will change. I'm personally OK about American Express and I'm happy to own it. Their position has been under attack for decades, more intensively lately, and will continue to be under attack. It's too big a business and it's too interesting a business and it could be too attractive a business for people to ignore it. It plays to the talents of some very smart people. It's a natural that a great many organizations that are really quite capable think about it and it's big.

**Charlie:** A lot of great businesses are not quite as great as they used to be. The packaged good business, the Procter & Gamble and the General Mills, they are all weaker than they used to be at their peak.

**Warren:** Auto companies.

**Charlie:** Oh my god, when I think of the power of General Motors when I was young. What happened was they wiped-out all the shareholders. I would no more have predicted that. When I was young, General Motors loomed over the economy like a colossus. It looked totally invincible with torrents of cash, torrents of everything.

**Warren:** Trying to hold down market share.

**Charlie:** Yes, because they were afraid they would be too monopolistic. So, the world changes. We can't make the portfolio change every time something is a little less advantaged than it used to be.

**Warren:** You have to be thinking all the time to see if something really changes the game in a big way. That's not only true for American Express, that's true for other things we own including things we own 100% of. We will be wrong sometimes, we will be late sometimes but we will be right sometimes too. It's not that we are not cognizant of threats, but assessing the probability of those threats being a minor problem or major problem, or a life-threatening problem is a tough game but that's what makes our job interesting.

**Charlie:** I think anybody in payments probably who is an established long time player with an old method has more danger than used to exist. There's just more fluidity in it.

**Warren:** Okay, Station 3.

## CATTLE INVESTING

**Q42. Shareholder, Station 3:** Hi Mr. Buffett, Hi Mr. Munger. I'm from Flagstaff Arizona, my name is Mick Kelly. My family runs some cattle ranches down in Arizona and that's what my question pertains to. I'm curious on your thoughts as it relates to the expanding global population in investing in cattle and if you think it's wise? Thank you.

**Warren:** Charlie?

**Charlie:** I think it's one of the worst businesses that I can imagine for somebody like us.

**Warren:** There's nothing personal about this.

**Charlie:** Not only is it a bad business, but we have no aptitude for it.

**Warren:** Some people have done well in it Charlie?

**Charlie:** Yeah, they have one good year every 20 years or something.

Questioner: I know you guys like steak.

Warren: Very much.

Charlie: But not owning cattle.

Warren: Actually, I know a few people that have done reasonably well in cattle. They usually own banks on the side or something. But I wish you the best in it. I'm in Kiewit Plaza if you want to send anything along.

Charlie: Somebody has to occupy the tough niches in the economy. We need you. [laughter].

Warren: Andrew.

## COMPENSATION INCENTIVES

Q43. Andrew Ross Sorkin: Warren and Charlie, well the first part for Charlie and the second part for Warren. Charlie, you clearly understand the power of incentives. How do you apply this at Berkshire when designing a compensation formula? Without naming names or dollar amounts please illustrate for us, with examples (a couple of examples), how Berkshire's operating managers get paid for performance in different industries?

The second part is for Warren. You once said you would write about how we should compensate

**the next Berkshire CEO. Can you describe exactly how we should do it now?**

**Charlie:** Warren would worry about the next CEO. When it comes to incentives, our incentive systems are quite different and what we try to adapt is the reality of each situation. The basic rule of incentives is you get what you're rewarded for. If you have a dumb incentive system, you get dumb outcomes. One of our really interesting incentive systems is at GEICO. I'll let Warren explain it to you because we don't have a normal profits type incentive for the people at GEICO. Warren, tell them because it's really interesting.

**Warren:** At GEICO, we have two variables. They apply to well over 20,000 people. I think you have to be there a year. Anyone that's been there a year or more (and I could be wrong on the exact period) is subject and knows and understands that these two variables will determine bonus compensation and as you go up the ladder, it has a multiplier effect. It's still the same two variables but it gets to be larger and larger in terms of bonus compensation as a percentage of your base. But it's always significant and those two variables are simple. I care about growing the business and I care about growing it with profitable businesses. We have a grid which consists of growth in policies in force, on one axis – not growth in dollars because that's reflected by average premiums which are outside their control – growth in policies in force. Then on the other gird, we have the profitability of the seasoned business. It costs a lot of money to put business on the books (we spend a lot of money on advertising and all of that). So, in the first year, any business we put on the books is going to reduce profits significantly. I don't want people to be worried about the profit that might be impaired by growing the business fast. So, profit of seasoned business and growth of policies in force, very simple. We've used it since 1995. We put a tiny little tweak or two in for new businesses or something. It's an overwhelmingly simple system and everybody understands it. In February or so it's a big day when the two variables are announced and people figure out how they come out on it. It totally aligns the goals of the organization in terms of compensation with the goals of the owner and that's a simple one.

**Charlie:** It's simple but other people might reward something like just profits. So, the people don't take on new businesses they should have taken on because it hurts profits. You need to think things through, and Warren is good at that and so is Tony Nicely.[27]

**Warren:** Just think about it, if someone came along and said "do you reward profits?" You don't want to reward profits alone. It would be the dumbest thing you could do. You just quit advertising and start shrinking the business a little. People know the very top person is getting paid based on the same two variables. They don't think the guys at the top have a

---

[27] Olza M. (Tony) Nicely is the Chairman and CEO of GEICO. Tony began his career at age 18 in 1961 as a clerk, and has been with the Company ever since.

cushy deal compared to them or all of that. It's just a very logical system. The interesting thing and I'll get to the second question in a minute. The interesting thing is if we brought in a compensation consultant, they would come up with plans designed for all of Berkshire or get us all pulling together.

**Charlie (interjecting):** Or may be an undertaking parlor. God knows where they get the plans.

**Warren:** The idea of having a sort of coordinated arrangement for incentive compensation across 70 or 80 businesses is totally nuts. And yet I will almost guarantee you that if we brought in somebody, they would be thinking in terms of some master plan and sub-plans and all that kind of thing and explain it with all kinds of objectives. We just try to figure out what makes sense in each business we are in. There are some businesses where the top person is enormously important and some businesses where the business itself dominates the result. We try to design plans that make sense. In certain cases, ... I asked one fellow to come to work for us – he wanted to sell his business. He had a business he wanted to sell but he also wanted to keep running it. The day I met him when he came to the office, I made a deal with him on it. I said, "Tell me what the compensation plan should be." He said, "I thought you told me that." I said, "No. I don't want a guy working for me that has a plan that he thinks doesn't makes sense or that he's unhappy with or chewing at him or he is complaining to his wife about it or whatever may be. You tell me what makes sense." He told me what he wanted; it made sense and we've been using it ever since. We never changed a word. We have so many different kinds of businesses. Some of them are very tough businesses, some are very easy businesses; some are capital intensive and some don't take capital. You just go up and down the line. To think that you will have a simple formula that can be sort of stamped out for the whole place and then with some overall stuff for corporate results on top of that, you would be wasting a lot of money, and you would be misdirecting incentives. We think it through one at a time and it seems to work out pretty well. In terms of the person that succeeds me, it is true I have sent two memos to the board with some thoughts on that. Maybe I will send a third one. I don't think it would be wise to disclose exactly what is in those letters. But it's the same principle as I've just gotten through describing.

**Charlie:** He [the questioner] wanted more bad examples. A lot of bad examples of incentives come from banking and investment banking. If you reward somebody with some share of the profits, and the profits are being reported using accounting practices that cause profits to exist on paper that are not really happening in terms of underlying economics then people are doing the wrong thing, and it's endangering the bank and hurting the country and everything else. That was a major part of the cause of the great financial crisis. The banks were reporting a lot of income they weren't making and the investment banks were too. The accounting rules allowed for a long time a lender to use, as his bad debt provisions, his previous historical loss rate. So, an idiot could make a lot of money by just making way gamier loans on high interest and accruing a lot of interest and saying, "I'm not going to lose any money on these loans since I didn't lose money on different loans in the past." That was insane for the accountants to allow that. Literally insane, that's not too strong a word and yet nobody is ashamed of it. I've never met an accountant that's ashamed of it.

**Warren:** Another possibility is when you get a very greedy chief executive who wants an enormous payoff for himself and to justify it, designs a pyramid so that a whole bunch of other people down the line get overpaid or get paid in relation to something they have no control over so that it doesn't look like he's all by himself in terms of the fantastic payoff he arranged for himself. There's a lot of misbehavior. You saw it in pricing of stock options. I literally would hear conversations in a boardroom where they hoped they were issuing the options at a terribly low price. Well, you get people interested in having options issued at terribly low prices, they may occasionally do something that might cause that. What could be dumber than a company looking for a way to issue shares at the lowest price? Compensation isn't as complicated as the world would like to make it. But if you were a consultant, you would want to make people think that it is very complicated and that only you could solve this terrible problem for them that they couldn't solve.

**Charlie:** We want it simple and right. We don't want it to reward what we don't want. Those of you with children, just imagine how your household would work if you constantly rewarded every child for bad behavior, the house would be ungovernable in short order.

**Warren:** Okay, Gregg.

## BNSF CAPITAL EXPENDITURES

**Q44. Gregg Warren: During the past several years Burlington Northern spent more than just about every railroad on capital expenditures. While the company reduced its CAPEX budget by $5.7 billion during 2015 to $4.3 billion this year, it still represents around 20% of annual revenue which we believe is, at least, the bare minimum for most railroads to continue to invest indefinitely. Other than maintenance CAPEX which is likely to account for around 60% of that total, what do you believe are the most likely additional investment opportunities for BNSF, realizing that the secular decline in coal (which has accelerated as of late), and the complicated nature of crude oil shipments, where BNSF has already invested heavily in the past few years, are likely to push it more towards other parts of the business?**

**Warren:** As I mention in the annual report, in the case of all railroads, merely spending their depreciation expense will not keep them in the same place. Depreciation is an inadequate measure of the actual steady state capital expenditure needs of a railroad. Even in these fairly non-inflationary ways (and that's an important consideration in buying the business), we knew that going in and it's been reinforced since. We spent a lot of money in 2015 because we had a lot of problems to correct. That was when we spent the $5.7 billion. I would say that the true maintenance CAPEX (if you're looking at $4.3 billion) is higher than 60% of that number when you really evaluate keeping the railroad in competitive shape to do just the same volume as it would be doing the year before. There is an additional expense at BNSF that is not reflected in the figures. We also have a lot of intangible expenses at some other businesses that aren't real expenses. I mean overall, I think that Berkshire's figures are actually on the conservative side in relation to real economic earnings. But that's not true at any railroad. We've also had something called positive train control which amounts to a lot of money for the industry. I think we may be a little further along than most of them in paying for that. But that's $200 million or $300 million dollars a year and maybe it will be close to $2 billion or something like that in aggregate. So, it is a very capital-intensive business. At BNSF, we run far more gross in revenue ton miles than any other railroad in North America. That has, obviously, some effect on capital expenditures. But I'd say that it's very likely that we will spend more than depreciation – unfortunately, quite a bit more than depreciation – to stay in the same place for a long, long time, as will other railroads. That's a negative in the picture. We will always be looking for ways to use capital expenditure money to develop additional business and we get that opportunity regularly. It's just a question of the size of it. We did a lot of that in the Bakken, and we got benefits from it. We are not getting as much benefits from it as we thought we would at this point when the price of oil has fallen off. But that was a very sensible capital expenditure and I hope we get the opportunity to do more. What's happening in coal with the decline, I mean, that doesn't really have anything to do with our overall capital expenditure budget except we won't be spending a whole lot of money to expand in that arena. Does that answer your question okay?

**Gregg:** I was just thinking that maybe within the model as well – if that's a longer-term opportunity to invest more heavily there.

**Warren:** We are always open to that. But you have to see a fair amount of revenue coming from it. We had a proposition very recently which we worked on for many years in terms of making the port considerably more efficient. We spent a lot of money on that and we spent a lot of time but we would have spent a whole lot more money, if it had been approved. Recently a court came out with a decision that was negative on it. Whether that kills the chance to do that or we look someplace else, we will have to look at the situation.

**Charlie:** Our competitors there pretend to be environmentalists. It's a common practice now.

**Warren:** In any event, we thought we had something that made a lot of sense for both the area and for the transportation system of the country.

**Charlie:** We were trying to do the right thing, and so far, we've lost.

**Warren:** But we are still willing to spend a lot of money if we can find things that make the railroad more efficient or make it larger, either way. Okay section 4.

## LOW CRUDE OIL PRICES

**Q45. Section 4, Shareholder: Good afternoon Mr. Buffett and Mr. Munger. My name is Marcus Douglas. I'm an investment advisor from Huston Texas. Where I'm from there are a lot of people losing their jobs, mostly due to the sharp decline of crude oil prices. My question pertains to the overall state of the union more so than my dear city. Keeping in mind that crude oil is primarily bought and sold in American dollars, do either of you believe the major fluctuations in the supply of crude oil influence the future monetary policy decisions?**

**Warren:** Well, that yours, Charlie.

**Charlie:** Well, my answer would be not much.

**Warren:** It's an important industry, obviously, and the decline in the price of oil has had a lot of effects.

It's very good for the consumer – hundreds of millions of consumers; and very bad for certain businesses like the one we bought in Lubrizol, and some others to a degree. Net, it should be good for the United States. Overall, we are a net oil importer. I mean it's just like it is good for the United States to have low prices for bananas because we are a banana importer. Anything we net buy is a plus when prices fall but oil is big enough and it extends into so many areas that it also hurts a lot of things when the price of oil falls. It particularly hurts capital value. The consumer gets the benefit when he or she goes to the filling station every 2 or 3 weeks or something like that and it comes in relatively small increments. The capital value contraction is huge, if you project out lower price oil for a while, and hits immediately. An oil field that was worth X may be worth ½ X or a third of X or no X overnight. So, there are certain big factors: in terms of our chemical operation, people just stop ordering immediately. So, you have this big impact on capital values immediately and you have the benefits move in overtime but, net, the United States is better off and Saudi Arabia is worse off when prices of oil are lower. Oil is a big part of the economy but our economy has continued to make progress overall during the oil price decline. But obviously different regions suffer disproportionately just like they boomed in the boom days. They got a real boom during the period when it was at 100 dollars and when fracking came in big time. Charlie?

**Charlie:** Well, I think that will do for this subject.

**Warren:** Okay, Carol.

## EXCESS CASH

**Q46. Carol Loomis:** This question comes from Larry Lebowitz of Boston. The year-end balance sheet for manufacturing service and retailing operations shows total current assets of $28.6 billion of which cash and equivalence are $6.8 billion. Meanwhile total current liabilities are $12.7 billion implying networking capital of $15.9 billion. It has become increasingly common for companies like Apple and Dell to finance their business via their suppliers, in some cases with negative working capital. Why is it necessary for these Berkshire businesses to have so much working capital, particularly so much cash? More generally, how do you think about efficiently managing the working capital of a business segment so large sprawling and decentralized as this one?

**Warren:** Well, we have excess cash at every place at Berkshire. So, at present, it doesn't really make any difference whether we have excess cash at certain subsidiaries or other subsidiaries. We have excess cash and as I've pointed out in the past, we will never go below $20 billion in cash and will actually stay comfortably above it. But, allowing for the preferreds of Kraft Heinz, we will again be over $60 billions of consolidated cash. We don't really worry much about what pocket it's in. It's not making anything anyway at these levels. Now if rates move higher, we've actually got the mechanics in process to do sweep accounts and that sort of things. I would pay no attention to the particular cash that is being held in that category. The cash in Berkshire Hathaway Energy and the cash in the railroad, we have independent levels that we don't guarantee their debt. They run with ample cash and we would not look at sweeping that down to a minimum. But if we talk about the forty or fifty of our miscellaneous subsidiaries, we will go to a sweep account when rates get to where it makes any difference to do it. Right now, when you're getting zero, it doesn't make much difference where you get the zero. I think the fella has overanalyzed it a little bit but I understand why he did it.

**Charlie:** Warren, one of his ideas is why don't we imitate some of these other people and pay our suppliers a lot more slowly so we have more working capital?

**Warren:** That's a big thing in business now. Last year Wal-Mart, for example, went to almost all of their suppliers, as I understand it - certainly the companies that we supply. They basically had a list of a half dozen things that they wanted the present suppliers to agree to and one of those things was more extended terms. Each of our companies made their own decisions. My guess is they got more extended terms from most of their suppliers maybe a very high percentage of their suppliers. I don't remember the exact request, whether they went from 30 days to 60 days, but they got a meaningful extension. In a couple of years or a year (it takes time to implement), you will see higher payables relative to sales at Wal-Mart than you saw a year or two ago. They are under a lot of pressure competing with Amazon and others and that's one of the ways they expressed it. I've seen it done at other places and it's conceivable that one of our subsidiaries might deem it wise to do it, but I don't think they will. I think the pressure for cash at Berkshire is not that high and I think the pressure or the desire for great relations with suppliers would probably overcome, in most of our managers' minds, any desire to start extending terms.

**Charlie:** I think it's hard to do that brutally when you're rich, and your supplier isn't and think that your supplier is going to love you. There's something to be said for leaning over backward to have a win-win relationship with both suppliers and customers, always.

**Warren:** It's never been pushed at Berkshire. You can argue we have a pretty good thing going in float anyways.

**Charlie:** Yeah, and we don't need it. Let someone else set the record on that one.

**Warren:** Okay, Johnny [Jonathan].

## LACK OF RESTRUCTURING CHARGES

**Q47. Jonathan Brandt:** Most American corporations separate out supposedly one-time restructuring costs whereas Berkshire doesn't. Berkshire's reported operating earnings are therefore in my opinion of higher quality. Have you ever calculated how much higher operating earnings on average would be if Berkshire separated out plant closing costs, product line exits, severance pay and similar items? Is it a martial number? Or does Berkshire not incur much in the way of these types of costs typically because most of your acquisitions are stand-alone?

**Charlie** [very quickly stepping in]: Let me take that one. That's a question like asking, "Why don't you kill your mother to get the insurance money?" We don't do it. We are not interested in manipulating those numbers. We haven't had a restructuring charge ever and I don't think we are about to start. [applause].

**Warren:** I will say this to Johnny. We don't do that. The numbers would not be huge. There could be a year, I suppose, when they might be for some reason. But they are more conservatively stated than most companies and I think they are of higher quality. But I pointed out also that I think our depreciation expense at the railroad which is standard (and which all the other railroads use) is inadequate as a measure of true operating earnings.

**Charlie:** And you're talking about it … we like to advertise our defects.

**Warren:** Not all of them. There's no question that we will have more amortization of certain intangibles which reduce earnings and reported earnings which in reality are not expenses. We will have more of that than some companies. I pointed out that I never want to report one of these things where I have the whole adjusted earnings and say this is what you're supposed to pay attention to because every one of those I've seen virtually results in some inflation of figures. Things are good enough at Berkshire that we don't need to inflate the figures. Okay, Station 5.

## CREDIT DEFAULT SWAPS

**Q48. Shareholder, Station 5: This is Martin Collin from Germany. I am a fixed income manager. We launched, with Henry Laborer, a fund.**

**Warren:** You have my sympathy.

**Questioner:** The volume is about $650 million; we are 4.1 percent ahead this year. Obviously, my question is about fixed income. If I look in your annual report it's a volume of about $25 billion and if I add, let's say, the CDS you were selling by the volume of $7 to $8 billion. So, my concrete question is the premium on your CDS is about 31 basis points at the end of the year. So, marked-to-market is probably at the high teens or at twenties. So, would you consider to unwind this position? Are you allowed to do it? But you probably can make exactly the contrary trade on it – that means you are buying protection. Is that a philosophy which you stand behind? Could you do that from ethical point of view when the premium is extremely low which is the case as the spreads are as I see it between 15 and 20 basis points.

**Warren:** We have one position left over from six or seven years ago (or thereabouts) that involves us selling protection on zero coupon municipal bonds with a nominal maturity value. Since they are zero coupons it's far off and not present value at all, I think $7.7 billion or something like that. We are just sitting with the position because we like the position. The gentleman mentions that our CDS – that's an insurance premium against our debt that people buy. There is a fair amount of activity in it from time to time. I think that's partially caused by the fact that we neither collateralized that municipal contract he refers to. But we don't collateralize, with minor exceptions, the equity puts that are still out there. So, the counterparties have to buy. I believe this is the case. I believe the counterparties have to buy protection on Berkshire's credit through CDS. Now, the people they buy it from, their credit probably isn't as good as Berkshire's, so it's probably an internal rule at some of the firms on the other side of the contract but that doesn't really make any difference to us. Back in 2008 and 2009, our CDS prices went up to a crazy level. I even commented here at the annual meeting that I'd love to be selling them myself except I wasn't allowed to. But what goes on in the CDS market really isn't of any particular interest to us. It's too bad for the other guys that they didn't ask for collateral from us or we would have given it to them. And they have to buy these things that like I say, from our standpoint, they are wasting their money; but they probably have internal rules that make them. I think I've addressed your question but Charlie do you think I've addressed his question?

**Charlie:** The truth of the matter is we don't pay much attention by trying to get an extra two basis points by being gamey on our short-term things. From my point of view, Credit Default position is a weird historical accident, and we don't pay much attention to it either. It will go away in due course.

**Warren:** All of our contracts are just going to expire. But we do a few operational contracts in our energy company – there's a couple of places where, for their own reasons, sometimes because the utility commissions want them to – they do certain things; but it's peanuts. The positions I instituted six or seven years ago are basically all in a runoff position and the first big runoffs will be in 2018, in couple of years.

**Charlie:** We are basically not in that. We don't fool around with our own credit default swaps.
A
**Warren:** No, never, but I would have liked to have sold them in 2008.

**Charlie:** I know, it's crazy.

**Warren:** People were paying 5% in terms of betting that Berkshire would go broke which was totally crazy. But I couldn't take advantage of it. I wanted to though. Becky.

## AJIT JAIN

**Q49. Becky Quick: This question comes from Tom Hinsley, a long-time shareholder from Huston, Texas who says: Over the years you've been effusive in your praise of Ajit Jain and his contributions to Berkshire. In the 2009 chairman's letter you wrote, "If Charlie, Ajit and I are ever sinking in a boat and you can only save one of us, swim to Ajit." My question is what if we don't get to Ajit in time? Please comment on the impact on National Indemnity and Berkshire [if we lost Ajit] and whether or not there's another Ajit in the house.**

**Warren:** There's not another Ajit in the house. I didn't hear the part immediately before " …there's another Ajit in the house."

**Becky:** The impact on National Indemnity. I guess the impact on the insurance companies as a result.

**Warren:** If we lost him?

**Becky:** Yes.

**Warren:** It would be very significant and that would be true of some other managers of some other subsidiaries. It's quite dramatic with Ajit's operation because, literally, there were a few years when we had like 25 or 30 people, where that operation, (it was an unusual period to be in) but where its earning potential under Ajit was fantastic. That probably won't happen to that degree again. I wish it would but he has done a tremendous amount for Berkshire. It started with Tony and there have been a lot of managers that have created billions and billions of value for Berkshire, and maybe you can get to the tens of billions. Having a fantastic manager that has a large potential business available to them and who makes the most of it, it's huge over time. You don't see it necessarily in a week or a month or anything that sort but when you're building capital value, … think of the value of Jeff Bezos to Amazon. I mean it wouldn't have happened without him. You are looking at huge values. I can name other situations. The value of Tom Murphy and Dan Burke was the difference between the 0 and what they ended up with. I mean they built that thing from a bankrupt UHF station. They didn't invent television or anything of that sort. They just managed it so well. So really outstanding managers are invaluable. We want to align ourselves with them. Charlie and I can't do it ourselves. We want to align ourselves with them and then have them feel about Berkshire the way we feel about it. If we do that then we have an enormous asset; and we do have it in Ajit and a number of the other managers. Charlie?

**Charlie:** Ajit has a longer shelf life than we do. He would be particularly missed.

**Warren:** Come on, let's not give up here, Charlie. [laughter]. I reject such defeatism. Cliff.

## FLOAT

**Q50. Cliff Gallant: Low to negative interest rates is something that's been discussed a few times today. You have mentioned its implications for return on float. I was wondering how should shareholders value the 25% of the float that's been created by retrocession reinsurance where the business is booked at an underwriting loss and at times has adversely developed?**

**Warren:** Cliff brings up some of our business in the insurance business. We take the probability of some underwriting loss in order to get to use the money for a very long period of time. It would look, with today's low interest rates, like we can't do much with that. There's two answers to that. For the duration of the kind of contracts we have, we don't expect these rates but we could be wrong. The second one also is that we do think that, occasionally, we will get chances, even in periods of low interest rates, to do things that will produce quite a bit very reasonable returns. We are not measuring it against double the corporates or anything of that sort. We are measuring it in the potential utility to us with our really pretty unusual flexibility in respect to the deployment of the funds and this long period, when we will have an opportunity perhaps to come up with one or two things where we can deploy money at a rate that may be quite a bit higher than other people assume now that money can be deployed. Charlie?

**Charlie:** We are willing to pay a little money now to have the certainty of having a lot of money available in case something really attractive comes up in a bit difficult time.

**Warren:** It's an option cost.

**Charlie:** It's an option cost, right.

**Warren:** The option came in handy in 2008-2009, for example.

**Charlie:** Did it ever!

**Warren:** Okay Station 6.

"And we don't want to talk about specific hits and failures."
Charlie Munger

"It's the way I see the world. It's a very interesting and very humorous place. Actually, I think Charlie has a better sense of humor than I have."
Warren Buffett

"I think if you see the world accurately, it's bound to be humorous because it's ridiculous."
Charlie Munger

# REAL ESTATE

**Q51. Shareholder, Station 6:** Hi Charlie and Warren. My name is Mindy Jensen and I'm from Longmont, Colorado. I work for the largest real estate investing social network online called BiggerPockets.com. We are seeing investors starting to get concerned that the real estate market is a bit frothy. Similar to the run-up of 2005, 6 and 7 that led to the crash in 2008. Warren, in 2012 you told Becky Quick that if you had a way to easily manage them you would buy 100,000 houses and rent them out. How do you feel about the real estate market today?

**Warren:** It is not as attractive as it was in 2012. We are not particularly better at predicting real estate markets than we are at stock markets or interest rate markets. But there are certainly – and it's driven to some extent by these low interest rates – but there are properties that being sold at very very low cap rates that strike me as having more potential for loss than gain. But then again, if you can borrow money for very little, and you think you're getting some very safe asset about 100 basis points or 150 basis points higher, there's a great temptation to do it. I think it's a mistake to do that, but you know, I could be wrong. I don't see a nationwide bubble in residential real estate now at all. I think in a place like Omaha, or most of the country, you are not paying bubble prices for residential real estate. But it's quite different than it was in 2012. I don't think the next time around the problem is going to be a real estate bubble. I think that it certainly was the cause in a very large part of what happened in 2008 and 9 but I don't think it will be a replica of that. Charlie?

**Charlie:** Nothing to add.

**Warren:** Andrew.

## INVESTMENTS BY TODD AND TED

**Q52. Andrew Ross Sorkin: Warren, Todd and Ted now have been at Berkshire for several years. What have been their biggest hits and failures specifically? And what have they learnt from Charlie and Warren and what are the biggest differences between you and them?**

**Warren:** I'll answer the last part because that's the easiest. I'm trying to think of very big deals that we can do something in, whether is in investments or in business, preferably just in operating businesses. Their primary job is working on investments – each has a $9 billion portfolio. One of them has, I don't know, perhaps 7 or 8 positions and the other one has may be 13 or 14. But they have a very similar approach to investing. They've both been enormously helpful in doing several things including important things for which they don't get paid a dime and which they are just as happy working on as they are when they are working on things that do pay off for them financially. They're perfect cultural fits for Berkshire. They are smart at what they do. They are a big addition to Berkshire. Charlie?

**Charlie:** Again, I've got nothing to add.

**Warren:** Did I cover the whole thing, Andrew or is there a part I missed?

**Andrew:** The biggest hits and failures. I think they specifically wanted to know in terms of investment, trying to understand the way they think and the way you think - are there differences?

**Warren:** I would say they have a bigger universe to work with. They can look at ideas in which they can put $500 million. I'm trying to think of ways to invest sums in the billions. They certainly have more extensive knowledge of certain industries and activities in business that have developed in the last 10-15 years; they would be smarter on that than I am. But their approach to investing – I mean they are looking for businesses that they understand through the stocks of those businesses that they can buy at a sensible price and they think will be earning significantly more money five or ten years from now. It's very similar to what I'm thinking about except probably I will add another 0 to it.

**Charlie:** And we don't want to talk about specific hits and failures.

**Warren:** No. We will never get into this disclosing. I mean we file reports every 90 days to show what Berkshire does in marketable securities. We don't identify … I may identify whether it's mine or theirs but we don't get into identifying what they do individually. Okay, Gregg.

## CASH IN THE FINANCE SEGMENT

**Q53. Gregg Warren:** Looking at Berkshires finance and financial products segment, there was a fairly significant increase in the amount of cash carried on the Group's books last year. After holding steady between $2 (billion) and $2.5 billion during 2012 to 2014, the amount of cash held at the segments spiked up to $5.4 billion at the end of the 3rd quarter last year and $7.1 billion dollars at the end of 2015. This incidentally coincided with your acquisition of GEs railcar leasing unit as well as the acquisition of several railcar repair maintenance facilities. Sales and profitability were fairly solid last year but don't really seem to account for the magnitude of change in cash. In investments, debt and other liabilities do not look to have changed significantly enough to account for the difference, perhaps accounting for about $1 billion of the increase. Just wondering where the additional 3.5 dollars in cash came from and whether or not the elevated level of cash at the end of last year is excess to the business or a new required level of cash to the operations.

**Warren:** I can't tell you where it came from. $3.5 billion, you think I would. But I can tell you why we were funneling money into the parent company and into the finance company. That money was basically dedicated to making the $22 billion portion of the Precision Castparts purchase that was accounted for by cash. We actually borrowed $12 billion but $10 billion of the borrowing was there. We pushed money from various sources depending on who owned what and that sort of thing. We pushed money into two of those entities and eventually into the parent company to take care of the $22 billion that was coming due at the end of January when Precision Castparts deal closed. There's really no significance other than that. Okay Station 7.

## IBM MOAT

**Q54. Shareholder, Station 7: Good afternoon Mr. Buffett and Mr. Munger. My name is Jeffery Estep form Cranford, New Jersey. I just have a simple question for you. How would you explain IBM's moat?**

**Warren:** I'm not sure that's a simple question.

**Charlie:** No, I don't know it either.

**Warren:** Well, it has certain strengths and certain weaknesses. I don't think we want to get into giving an investment analysis of any of the portfolio companies that we own. I think I probably better leave it there. Charlie?

**Charlie:** Yeah, it's obviously coping with considerable change in the computing world and it's attempting something that's big and interesting. God knows whether it will work modestly or very well. I don't think Warren knows either.

**Warren:** No, we will find out whether the strengths are strengths.

**Charlie:** It's a field that a lot of intelligent people are trying to get big in.

**Warren:** Okay we are going to go to section 8 then we will adjourn for 15 minutes prior to the formal meeting of the company.

## SENSE OF HUMOR

**Q55. Section 8, Shareholder: Hello everybody, good afternoon. My name is Christian Campos. I'm from New York City. I am a senior accounting major at Baruch College part of the City University of New York. Mr. Buffett, in your annual shareholder letters and during interviews, and even today, your sense of humor always shines through. Where does your sense of humor come from? Please tell us. Thank you.**

**Warren:** It's the way I see the world. It's a very interesting and at times very humorous place. Actually, I think Charlie has a better sense of humor than I have. So, I will let him answer where he got his.

**Charlie:** I think if you see the world accurately, it's bound to be humorous because it's ridiculous. [applause].

**Warren:** Well, I think that's a good note to close on. We will reconvene in 15 minutes for the formal part of the meeting. We have one proxy item to act on. So I hope those of you who are interested in learning more about – actually, the insurance aspect of - climate change will stick around. We will have a discussion on that then. I will see you at 3:45. Thank you. [applause].

## End of Q&A session

# Epilogue

If you regularly read the writings of Warren Buffett and Charlie Munger and pay attention to their teachings on life and business, there is no question that the only outcome will be to grow in wisdom. Their combination of high ethical standards and astute business acumen is rare. As aptly stated by Bill Gates, a member of the Berkshire Hathaway board, the weekend of the AGM "is one of the most enjoyable 'duties' of my year."[28] We agree. Attending Berkshire Hathaway shareholders' meeting is one of the best ways to spend a weekend. We consider Warren Buffett's letters to the shareholders and their (Warren's and Charlie's) answers to the questions at the AGM as the best lessons in finance and investment.

You are probably reading this book because you see yourself as a student of value investing, specifically registered in the school of Warren Buffett and Charlie Munger. We hope if you attended the 2016 shareholders' meeting, this book has been a refresher and you now have a record of it so that you can revisit Warren's and Charlie's perspectives on the questions that were asked. If you were not able to attend the meeting, then this is your access to the Q&A session. We hope this format will continue and we will continue to learn from these legends.

---

[28]    http://www.gatesnotes.com/About-Bill-Gates/Master-Class-with-Warren-Buffett-Berkshire-Hathaway-Annual-Meeting-2014

We expect the 2017 meeting to be equally informative, enlightening, fascinating, and fun. While we have no idea what questions will be asked, we expect people to be curious about decisions such as getting into airline stocks; the public relations problems with United Airlines in particular; Warren and Charlie's take on recent events at Wells Fargo regarding the bogus accounts; their views and expectations on President Donald Trump's stand on environmental issues, especially regarding clean energy; etc. It is definitely worth attending and we encourage all shareholders who can to attend.

As always, we expect investment wisdom that is certainly worth keeping record of. Warren and Charlie always have unusual but accurate perspectives of business and finance and it will be worth your while to hear them in their own words. We will continue to do our best to take accurate notes and to present them in a reader-friendly form.

# About the Authors

## Eben Otuteye

Eben Otuteye is Professor of Finance at the University of New Brunswick, Fredericton, Canada. Professor Otuteye joined the Faculty of Business Administration at UNB in 1987 where he has been teaching various finance courses, including principles of finance, corporate finance, investments, value investing, personal financial planning, and theory of finance, in both the BBA and MBA programs.

Dr. Otuteye's research interests include behavioral finance, value investing, asset pricing models, portfolio management strategies, and the economics of e-business, topics on which he has made many conference presentations all over the world and published in several high-ranking journals.

In collaboration with Mohammad Siddiquee, Professor Otuteye developed a heuristic (the O-S heuristic) for making value investing decisions. This is a system that incorporates the value investing principles as originally propounded by Benjamin Graham and its extensions as developed and practiced by Warren Buffett and Charlie Munger.

## Mohammad Siddiquee

Mohammad Siddiquee is an Assistant Professor of Finance at the University of New Brunswick Saint John. Dr. Siddiquee studies behavioral finance as well as the psychology of decision making in investment management.

Influenced by the works of Benjamin Graham and his disciple Warren Buffett, he is also studying value investing. Dr. Siddiquee is currently collaborating with Dr. Otuteye on a project "Redefining Risk in Common Stock Investment from a Value Investing Perspective," which may lead to rethinking traditional risk-return paradigms.

Dr. Siddiquee taught managerial finance, investment and portfolio management, and personal financial planning in the undergraduate program, and corporate finance and entrepreneurial finance in the MBA program. Dr. Siddiquee has developed and teaches a class, *A Master Class with Warren Buffett* in the summer. He is an avid value investor.

# INDEX